SANCTIONS, DIPLOMACY, AND INFORMATION: PRESSURING NORTH KOREA

HEARING

BEFORE THE

COMMITTEE ON FOREIGN AFFAIRS
HOUSE OF REPRESENTATIVES

ONE HUNDRED FIFTEENTH CONGRESS

FIRST SESSION

SEPTEMBER 12, 2017

Serial No. 115–91

Printed for the use of the Committee on Foreign Affairs

Available via the World Wide Web: http://www.foreignaffairs.house.gov/ or
http://www.gpo.gov/fdsys/

U.S. GOVERNMENT PUBLISHING OFFICE

26–836PDF WASHINGTON : 2018

CONTENTS

Page

WITNESSES

Ms. Susan A. Thornton, Acting Assistant Secretary, Bureau of East Asian and Pacific Affairs, U.S. Department of State 5

The Honorable Marshall Billingslea, Assistant Secretary, Office of Terrorism and Financial Intelligence, U.S. Department of the Treasury 12

LETTERS, STATEMENTS, ETC., SUBMITTED FOR THE HEARING

Ms. Susan A. Thornton: Prepared statement 8

The Honorable Marshall Billingslea: Prepared statement 15

APPENDIX

Hearing notice 56

Hearing minutes 57

The Honorable Gerald E. Connolly, a Representative in Congress from the Commonwealth of Virginia: Prepared statement 59

Questions submitted for the record by the Honorable Eliot L. Engel, a Representative in Congress from the State of New York, and responses from:

Ms. Susan A. Thornton 61

The Honorable Marshall Billingslea 67

Questions submitted for the record by the Honorable Ami Bera, a Representative in Congress from the State of California, and responses from:

Ms. Susan A. Thornton 72

The Honorable Marshall Billingslea 75

Questions submitted for the record by the Honorable Ann Wagner, a Representative in Congress from the State of Missouri, and responses from:

Ms. Susan A. Thornton 78

The Honorable Marshall Billingslea 80

Questions submitted for the record by the Honorable Bradley S. Schneider, a Representative in Congress from the State of Illinois, and responses from:

Ms. Susan A. Thornton 81

The Honorable Marshall Billingslea 82

SANCTIONS, DIPLOMACY, AND INFORMATION: PRESSURING NORTH KOREA

TUESDAY, SEPTEMBER 12, 2017

House of Representatives,
Committee on Foreign Affairs,
Washington, DC.

The committee met, pursuant to notice, at 10:05 a.m., in room 2172, Rayburn House Office Building, Hon. Ed Royce (chairman of the committee) presiding.

Chairman ROYCE. Before we gavel the hearing in, I would just like to remind audience members that disruption of committee proceedings is against the law and will not be tolerated. Although, wearing themed shirts while seated in the hearing room is certainly permissible, holding up signs during the proceedings, that is not permissible. So any disruptions will result in a suspension of the proceedings until the Capitol Police can restore order.

With that, I would like to call us to order here for our hearing this morning, and ask all the members to take their seats, if you could. On September 3rd, North Korea detonated a nuclear device that, according to news reports, was stronger than all of its previous tests combined. This hydrogen bomb represents the latest advancement in North Korea's long-running nuclear and intercontinental ballistic missile program, which now pose an urgent threat to the United States. Moreover, the apparent speed in which these North Korean advancements have occurred are challenging the security structure across East Asia, creating dangerous instability in the region, and that instability we will likely be dealing with for decades to come.

So today, this committee is going to discuss the tools that must be deployed and fully utilized to address these threats. And I believe the response from the United States and our allies should be supercharged. We need to use every ounce of leverage. When I had breakfast this morning with Secretary Tillerson, we laid out these issues. That leverage includes sanctions, it includes diplomacy, it includes projecting information into North Korea to put maximum pressure on this rogue regime. Time is running out.

And let us be clear, sanctions can still have an important impact. North Korea's advanced weapons programs rely on foreign-sourced technology. Much of these programs are made outside the country. North Korea pays an inordinate amount of money, and it has to have hard currency to do it, to run this very expensive ICBM program and this nuclear weapons program. Since it requires hard currency, that is the Achilles heel. Unfortunately, years have been wasted as sanctions have been weak, allowing North Korea to access financial resources and build its nuclear and missile programs. Any sanction that crimps North Korea's access to technology is urgently needed.

Congress has done its part to ramp up economic pressure. We passed a North Korea Sanctions bill last February, authored by myself and Mr. Eliot Engel, our ranking member. In July, we increased the tools at the administration's disposal, as part of the big sanctions package that we passed here, including sanctions on North Korea and Russia and the Iran missile program. Part of that included targeting North Korean slave labor exports. Part of it, again, refined some of the focus on banking. And part of it, also, was focused on exports to ports around the world from North Korea.

In August, the administration secured a major victory with the unanimous adoption of U.N. Security Council Resolution 2371, which Ambassador Haley called "the strongest sanctions ever imposed in response to a ballistic missile test." She is now hard at work on another resolution.

To be effective, these tools need to be implemented aggressively. The administration deserves credit for increasing the pace of designations. And I appreciate Treasury Secretary Mnuchin's statements that more are coming. But we need to dramatically ramp up the number of North Korea-related designations.

These designations do not require Beijing's cooperation. We can designate Chinese banks and companies unilaterally, giving them a choice between doing business with North Korea or the United States. And I would just observe that not doing business with the United States for many of these companies would risk bankruptcy for these institutions.

Earlier this year, Treasury sanctioned the Bank of Dandong, a regional Chinese bank. And that is a good start. But we must target major Chinese banks doing business with North Korea, such as China Merchants Bank, and even big state-owned banks, like the Agricultural Bank of China. They have a significant presence in the United States. And if they do not stop doing business with North Korea, they should be sanctioned now.

It is not just China, we should go after banks and companies in any countries that do business with North Korea the same way. Just as we pressed China to enforce U.N. sanctions banning imports of North Korea coal and iron and seafood, we should press countries to end all trade with North Korea. This grave nuclear risk demands it.

Sanctions are not the only way to apply pressure on the regime. We must maintain a united front with our allies. I just returned from South Korea where people are on edge. We were there when the missile was launched over Japan. It doesn't matter if you are talking to government officials there, or the business community, or the average person on the street; they all understand the threat. So I am pleased that the THAAD missile defense system has been fully deployed. I am also pleased that the administration is strengthening regional deterrence through additional U.S. armed sales to Japan and South Korea, which we discussed this morning.

Finally, we need to do much better at getting information into North Korea so that North Koreans can better understand the brutality and corruption of the self-serving Kim regime. And these efforts are already pressuring the regime, creating some unrest and increasing defections from North Korea. But I am afraid our efforts here grade poorly. International broadcasting and fomenting dissent just have not been a priority, and that is unacceptable in this situation. While we should take a diplomatic approach to North Korea, the reality is that this regime will never be at peace with its people, its neighbors, or us, and now is the time to apply that pressure.

With that said, let me turn to the ranking member of our committee, Mr. Eliot Engel of New York.

Mr. ENGEL. Mr. Chairman, thank you for calling this hearing. You and I have worked together for a long time on the Korean situation. We had a hearing on this topic to start the year. This committee works in a bipartisan manner to advance some of the toughest sanctions ever on North Korea, which are now U.S. law.

Yesterday the United Nations Security Council unanimously agreed to Resolution 2375, in response to the Kim regime's sixth nuclear test. And we are revisiting the threat of North Korea today so we can hear directly from the administration.

Mr. Chairman, I am grateful for your unwavering leadership on this issue. To our witnesses, welcome to the for Foreign Affairs Committee and thank you for your service.

Acting Assistant Secretary Thornton, I have tremendous confidence in you and our career diplomats, but it is hard to believe that nearly 8 months into this administration, there is no nominee for Assistant Secretary for East Asian and Pacific Affairs. The same goes for Ambassador to South Korea, Under Secretary for Arms Control and International Security, and a range of other senior State Department officials. This administration has said that North Korea is its top foreign policy priority; but between the President's dangerous and irresponsible communication on the matter, and the inexplicable reluctance to get personnel in place, he is, in my opinion, undercutting his own peaceful pressure strategy.

I view the Kim regime's nuclear program as the single greatest threat to American national security and to global security. Right now, we need all hands on deck and focused on the same objective. We do that here in this committee. But that objective, of course, also gets to one of the main questions. While we all share the desire to rid North Korea of nuclear weapons, some have said that Kim will never give them up regardless of the pressure.

I have been to North Korea twice, Mr. Chairman, as you know, and I can tell you and everybody else, that this is not a regime that looks at the world the way any other government does. The Kim regime is bent on self-preservation above all else and is very willing to sacrifice their own people to achieve that end. That makes them obviously incredibly dangerous. The military options in the North Korea contingency are incredibly grim and it is hard to overstate just how devastating a conflict on the Korean peninsula would be. If this conflict escalates into a war, we could be measuring the cost in millions of lives lost.

Time is clearly running out. Once the regime in Pyongyang possesses nuclear weapons that can strike the United States, it will immediately raise questions about the reliability of our security commitments to our alliance partners, Japan and South Korea. Nuclear capabilities of this kind would likely embolden the North Koreans to engage in other bad behavior, such as harassment of our allies and continued proliferation of nuclear technologies. Some even speculate that the Kim regime might even seek reunification of the peninsula on its own terms.

So we need a smart strategy, first of all, and then definitely consistent execution of that strategy, and obviously, that is no easy task. Administrations of both parties were unable to put a stop to North Korea's nuclear program. North Korea detonated its first nuclear weapon in 2006, and a few years later the Bush administration removed North Korea from the State sponsor of terrorism list as an inducement to join the Six-Party talks.

Since Kim Jong Un assumed power, bomb and missile tests have increased in frequency. And this year, since the start of the Trump administration, we have seen an alarming increase in the frequency and the significance of tests, and of course, the detonation a few weeks ago of what appears to be a thermonuclear device.

So where do we go from here? Personally, I agree with Secretary of Defense Mattis that we are "never out of diplomatic solutions when it comes from North Korea," although, I am not sure President Trump shares that view. Frankly, I am not sure he even knows what his views are on this. At present, however, Kim Jong Un doesn't seem to be anywhere close to sitting down for talks of any kind, much less sincere negotiations.

The first order of business should be to have a moratorium on testing, to halt the progress of North Korea's nuclear program. Our objective has long been a denuclearized North Korea, and we cannot lose sight of that aim. In my view, we have not exhausted economic pressure through sanctions, and we need to do all we can to keep pressure up on the Kim regime. But at the same time we increase pressure, we must also ramp up coordination with our allies. We must demonstrate that defensive military measures are at the ready, both to reassure our allies and to deter the regime from any action that could lead to deadly escalation.

I am interested in hearing from our witnesses today about how we are going to pursue those aims. Under ordinary circumstances, I would say this is a tall order. But I have to say again, the President's behavior surrounding this crisis is making the situation even more challenging. Outrageous red lines like threats of fire and fury, shaming our allies through tweets, inconsistently from one day to the next about Kim Jong Un or China or economic partnership with South Korea, picking a fight with South Korea right at this time, loose talk about expanding America's nuclear arsenal, and the proliferation of these devastating weapons. All these actions undermine the credibility of the Office of the President, and the credibility of the U.S. Government, effectively undermining U.S. leadership, and driving a wedge between Washington and our friends, creating grave uncertainty with China, whose cooperation we need, and with North Korea, whose leader is, as we know, single-minded and ruthless.

Our country faces a serious national security challenge, and we need principled and visionary leadership. We need to be standing with our allies, acting with integrity, and reaffirming our commitments. The President needs to lead on the global stage, pushing China and Russia to enforce sanctions effectively, and building consent is about a path forward, not waiting to see who does what next and then reacting with the first words that come to mind.

So I look forward to hearing from our witnesses about what American leadership should look like in this crisis, and how we find the right path forward. I thank you again, Mr. Chairman, and I yield back.

Chairman ROYCE. Thank you. This morning we are pleased to be joined by a distinguished panel. We have with us Ms. Susan Thornton, Acting Assistant Secretary in the Bureau of East Asian Affairs at the Department of State. And as a career member of the foreign service, she has spent the last 20 years working on U.S. policy in Europe and Asia, focused on the countries of the former Soviet Union and on East Asia.

Assistant Secretary Marshall Billingslea is the Assistant Secretary in the Office of Terrorism and Financial Intelligence at the Department of the Treasury. Mr. Billingslea previously served as managing director of business intelligence services for Deloitte, where we focused on illicit finance. So we welcome both our witnesses to the committee.

Without objection, the witnesses' full, prepared statements are going to be made part of the record. And all members here are going to have 5 calendar days to submit any statements or any additional questions of you, or any extraneous material for the record. And with that, I would just suggest—and we will begin with you, Assistant Secretary Thornton. If you could summarize your remarks, and then we will go to Mr. Billingslea, and then we will go to questions.

STATEMENT OF MS. SUSAN A. THORNTON, ACTING ASSISTANT SECRETARY, BUREAU OF EAST ASIAN AND PACIFIC AFFAIRS, U.S. DEPARTMENT OF STATE

Ms. THORNTON. Thank you very much, Mr. Chairman. Chairman Royce, Ranking Member Engel, members of the committee, thank you so much for the opportunity to appear before you today to discuss the ever-increasing challenge that North Korea poses. The threat posed by North Korea's ballistic missile and nuclear program is grave.

North Korea's sixth nuclear test on September 3 is an unacceptable provocation that ignores repeated calls from the international community for a change in their behavior. It followed the August 28 ballistic missile launch that overflew portions of Hokkaido, Japan, and two ICBM launches in July. These provocations represent a tangible threat to the security of Japan and South Korea, our allies, and to the entire globe. We cannot allow such flagrant violations of international law to continue.

North Korea has also made dramatic threats regarding its ability to hit Guam and other parts of the United States. Secretary of Defense Mattis has made clear that we have the ability to defend ourselves and our allies from any attack, and that our commitments to our allies remain iron clad. This administration, though, has developed a clear strategy of applying international pressure to hold Pyongyang to account.

First, we continue to push for strong U.N. sanctions. Last night the U.N. Security Council passed another significant set of international sanctions, the second set of sanctions in the last 2 months, unanimously adopted by the U.N. Security Council.

Second, we are using our domestic laws to impose sanctions on individuals and entities that enable the DPRK's illicit activities.

Third, we are pressing countries to fully implement the U.N. Security Council resolutions and sanctions, and to harmonize their domestic sanctions regimes with those Security Council designations.

Fourth, we are urging the international community to cease normal political interactions with the DPRK, and increase its diplomatic isolation.

And, fifth, we are calling on countries to cut trade ties with Pyongyang to choke off revenue sources that finance the regime's weapons programs. Even as we pursue denuclearization on the Korean peninsula, deterrence, as was mentioned by the ranking member, is an essential part of our strategy. We have deployed the THAAD anti-missile system to the Republic of Korea, and continue to take other measures to prepare ourselves to respond to any DPRK attack, whether on the United States, South Korea, or Japan, with overwhelming force.

We have been clear, we are not seeking regime change or collapse in North Korea, and we do not seek accelerated reunification, or an excuse to send troops north of the demilitarized zone. We do seek peaceful denuclearization of the Korean peninsula, and a North Korea that stops belligerent actions and is not presenting a threat to the United States or our allies.

We recognize that the success of this pressure strategy will depend on cooperation from international partners, especially China. And we are clear-eyed in viewing China's growing, if uneven support, for international measures against the DPRK. China has taken some notable steps on implementing sanctions, but we would like to see them do more.

We continue to engage with China and Russia to further pressure the DPRK, but if they do not act, we will use the tools at our disposal. Just last month, we rolled out new sanctions targeting Russian and Chinese individuals and entities that were doing illicit trade with North Korea. So while there is more work to be done, we do see encouraging signs of progress on increasing the pressure on the North Korean regime.

Countries spanning the globe have issued strong statements against the ICBM test and the most recent nuclear test. We have seen countries expel sanctions, North Korean officials, prevent certain individuals from entering their jurisdictions, reduce the size of North Korean diplomatic missions in their countries, and cancel or downgrade diplomatic engagements or exchanges.

Just in the recent days, we have had two announcements by two countries, Mexico and Egypt, about their efforts to downgrade relations with North Korea. Countries have halted visa issuances to North Korean laborers and are phasing out the use of these workers. South Korea, Japan, and Australia have implemented unilateral national sanctions against targeted entities and individuals, and European partners are collaborating with us on maximizing pressure on the DPRK.

Unfortunately, despite all of this, we have yet to see a notable change in the DPRK's dangerous behavior or signs that it is interested in credible talks on denuclearization. We will continue to step up efforts to sanction individuals and entitles, enabling the DPRK regime and its weapons programs. Following the nuclear test, we are pressing hard for a new Security Council resolution, which, of course, was adopted last night. And we hope that these new sectoral sanctions, including textiles, provisions on oil, provisions on shipping, et cetera, will allow us to increase our pressure.

China and Russia should continue to exert their unique leverage, of course, on the DPRK. And it should be clear that we will never accept North Korea as a nuclear state. We will continue to work within our alliances to develop additional defense measures to protect the people of the United States, and also of our allies. And at the same time, we will not lose sight of the plight of the three remaining U.S. citizens who have been unjustly detained by North Korea, nor of the regime's egregious human rights violations.

We will continue to reiterate our willingness to resolve this issue through diplomacy. And if the DPRK indicates an interest in serious engagement, we will explore that option, but with clear eyes about the DPRK's past track record of violating negotiated agreements.

Thank you, again, for letting me testify today, and I am looking forward to your questions.

[The prepared statement of Ms. Thornton follows:]

Statement of Susan Thornton
Acting Assistant Secretary
Bureau of East Asian and Pacific Affairs
U.S. Department of State
Before the House of Foreign Affairs Committee
September 12, 2017

North Korea Policy

Chairman Royce, Ranking Member Engel, and Members of the Committee:
Thank you for the opportunity to appear before you today for this timely hearing on North
Korea. Thank you also for your attention to the North Korea threat and how the United States is
addressing it.

The threat posed by North Korea's ballistic missile and nuclear weapons and other weapons of
mass destruction (WMD) program is gravely serious, and one that warrants immediate and
urgent attention, as this Administration has provided. The test of a nuclear device on September
3, North Korea's sixth nuclear test, is an unacceptable provocation that ignores repeated calls
from the international community for a change in North Korea's behavior. It followed the
August 28 ballistic missile launch that overflew portions of Hokkaido, which underscored the
direct threat posed by Pyongyang's missile and nuclear programs. It is the first declared ballistic
missile overflight of Japan, and represents a clear and tangible threat to the security of Japan and
the entire East Asia region. Let me emphasize that we continue to stand with our allies, Japan
and South Korea, in the face of this escalating threat.

Since the beginning of 2017 alone, North Korea has launched more than fifteen ballistic missiles
into the seas around it, including two ICBMs. In 2016 it tested two nuclear devices. And of
course, North Korea has made a number of dramatic threats regarding its ability to hit specific
targets including Guam and other parts of the United States. Secretary of Defense Mattis has
made clear that we have the ability to defend ourselves and our allies – South Korea and Japan –
from any attack and that our commitments to our allies remain ironclad.

We cannot allow such flagrant violations of international law to continue. We must hold
Pyongyang to account.

This administration has developed a clear strategy for doing just that. The strategy involves
forging an all-encompassing international coalition to apply diplomatic, economic, and political
pressure on North Korea to bring the regime to understand the only path to peace, prosperity and
international acceptance is to cease its provocative actions and to abandon its destabilizing
missile and nuclear programs.

We have used different monikers for this strategy – "maximum pressure," "peaceful pressure,"
and "strategic accountability," but the strategy's components are the same: (1) We continue to
push for strong multilateral sanctions against the DPRK at the United Nations. Through this
forum, we are galvanizing the international community to stand together in rebuke of North
Korea's belligerent acts and to pressure Pyongyang to abandon its unlawful programs. (2) We

are using the authorities granted in our domestic law under the North Korean Sanctions and Policy Enhancement Act and the new authorities under the Countering America's Adversaries Through Sanctions Act to impose sanctions on individuals and entities that enable the DPRK's illicit activities, deterring such conduct and sending a strong signal to the regime that we're watching their movements. (3) We continue to press countries around the world to fully implement UN Security Council Resolutions against North Korea – including UNSCRs 2270, 2321, 2356, and 2371, and to consider harmonizing their domestic sanction regimes with our designations on North Korean and third-country entities (4) Likewise, we continue to urge the international community to cease normal political interactions with the DPRK, including by suspending or downgrading diplomatic relations with North Korea and ending diplomatic visits and exchanges. (5) Finally, we continue to call for all countries to cut trade ties with Pyongyang to increase North Korea's financial isolation and choke off revenue sources – both licit and illicit – that finance the regime's weapons programs.

Even as we pursue denuclearization, deterrence is also a central part of our DPRK strategy. We are fully committed to the defense of the United States and our allies and are ready to respond to any DPRK attack. We have partially deployed THAAD to the ROK and continue to take other measures to prepare ourselves, South Korea, and Japan to respond to any DPRK attack with overwhelming force. We must be unequivocal in our messaging to North Korea that any attack on the United States or our allies will be met with an overwhelming response.

Throughout our execution of this strategy, we have been clear about what our strategy is not: We are not seeking regime change or collapse. Nor do we seek an accelerated reunification of Korea, or an excuse to send troops north of the Armistice Agreement's Military Demarcation Line. We have no desire to inflict harm on the long-suffering North Korean people, whom we view as distinct from the hostile regime in Pyongyang.

We recognize that the success of the pressure strategy will depend on cooperation from international partners, especially Beijing. We are working closely with China to execute this strategy and are clear-eyed in viewing the progress – growing if uneven – that China has made on this front. We are conferring closely with our Chinese counterparts to ensure strict implementation of China's commitment to curb imports of North Korean coal, iron, iron ore, lead and lead ore, and seafood. If fully implemented UNSCR 2371's ban on these items could substantially reduce DPRK revenues this year from the $1.5 billion North Korea earned from the export of these items to China in 2016.

We continue to work with China and Russia to improve the implementation of sanctions, but there is more to be done. Secretary Tillerson said it best when he called China's support for the pressure campaign "notable, but uneven." We hope to work with China and Russia to resolve this issue and will continue to engage in a dialogue on how to further pressure the DPRK. We have also made clear that if China and Russia do not act, we will use the tools we have at our disposal. Just last month we rolled out new sanctions targeting Russian and Chinese individuals and entities supporting the DPRK. We will continue to take action multilaterally and unilaterally to disrupt North Korea's illicit activities wherever they are located.

Signs of Progress

While there is more work to be done, we see encouraging signs of progress from our partners around the globe on increasing pressure on North Korea:

- Countries spanning all regions of the globe issued strong statements against the DPRK's July 3 and July 28 intercontinental ballistic missile (ICBM) tests, as well as the most recent launches and the September 3 nuclear test. These include countries that have not traditionally aligned with the United States on this matter – countries like Mexico and Sudan.

- We have seen countries expel sanctioned North Korean officials and North Korean diplomats engaged in illicit commercial or arms-related activities, and prevented certain North Korean individuals from entering or transiting their jurisdictions.

- Countries have reduced the size of the North Korean diplomatic mission in their countries, and canceled or downgraded diplomatic engagements or exchanges with North Korea. For example, Peru and Kuwait are two of several countries that reduced the size of the North Korean embassies they host.

- Across the globe, countries are beginning to view visiting North Korean official delegations with caution, recognizing that welcoming these delegations not only lends tacit support to North Korea's nuclear and ballistic missiles programs, but comes at a cost to their international reputation and relations with the United States and others.

- Countries in the Middle East, Europe, and Southeast Asia halted visa issuances to North Korean laborers and are phasing out the use of these workers, whose wages are garnished to fund the regime and its unlawful nuclear and missile programs. Malaysia deported hundreds of DPRK workers and suspended issuing further work permits.

- Other countries, such as the Republic of Korea (ROK), Japan, and Australia have implemented their own unilateral sanctions on entities violating UN sanctions. EU partners are augmenting autonomous restrictive measures to implement UN Security Council resolutions, and key European partners, particularly the UK, France, and Germany, are collaborating with us on maximizing pressure on the DPRK.

- Countries have tightened restrictions on the DPRK's ability to use its diplomatic missions to generate revenue. For example, Germany is shutting down a hostel located on DPRK embassy grounds in Berlin.

- On August 5, ASEAN Foreign Ministers issued their strongest statement to date in response to the DPRK's ICBM launch. Their joint statement expressed "grave concern" over the escalation of tensions and recent missile tests, expressed commitment to a denuclearized Korean Peninsula, and urged the DPRK to comply immediately with all relevant UNSC resolutions. We welcomed this strong, principled statement ahead of UNSCR 2371.

Next Steps

Unfortunately, despite the way the international community has come together to pressure the DPRK, we have yet to see a notable change in DPRK's dangerous behavior or any signs that it is willing or interested in credible talks on denuclearization at this stage. Our military, together with our allies, remains prepared to respond immediately and resolutely to any attack or threat of attack. There should be no doubt about our resolve to defend our allies and our homeland. We will not ape Pyongyang's well-honed practice of carelessly and needlessly escalating tensions, but we are ready to respond if necessary. Meanwhile, we remain open to diplomacy, but the DPRK must show it is ready for serious engagement. We have not seen any such indication. In fact, each ballistic missile launch from North Korea – to say nothing of its most recent nuclear test – only signals the opposite. As a result, we will continue to urge countries around the world to take actions to make clear to the DPRK that its behavior is intolerable, and continue to build pressure.

We will step up efforts to sanction individuals and entities enabling the DPRK regime, irrespective of location or nationality. Following the nuclear test, we are pressing hard for a new Security Council Resolution, which we hope will include new sectoral sanctions, including oil, textiles, and workers. Countries like China and Russia must continue to exert their unique leverage over the DPRK. We will never recognize North Korea as a nuclear state.

We will continue to stand with our allies in the region and will work with Japan and South Korea. We are enhancing U.S.-Japan-ROK trilateral diplomatic and security cooperation. We will continue to work within our alliances to develop additional defense measures to answer the threat posed by the DPRK's nuclear and ballistic missile programs, and to protect the people of the United States, Japan, and the Republic Korea. Third parties will not deter us from taking appropriate defensive measures in the face of the DPRK's growing security challenge.

While addressing the nuclear and ballistic missile threat is our most pressing issue, we have not and will not lose sight of the plight of the three remaining U.S. citizens who have been unjustly detained by North Korea nor of the regime's egregious human rights violations. Due to mounting concerns over the serious risk of arrest and long-term detention, the Department imposed a travel restriction on all U.S. nationals' use of a passport to travel in, through, or to North Korea which went into force September 1. We seek to prevent the future detentions of U.S. citizens by the North Korean regime to avoid another tragedy like that which Otto Warmbier and his family endured. We will continue to press for accountability for those involved in such deplorable abuses.

We will also continue to reiterate our willingness to solve this issue through diplomacy. If the DPRK indicates an interest in serious engagement, we will explore that option, but we will do so with clear eyes about the DPRK's past track record of violating the spirit and the letter of negotiated agreements.

We appreciate the strong interest in this issue from Congress, and we look forward to continuing our cooperation. Thank you for inviting me to testify today. I am pleased to answer any questions you may have.

———————

STATEMENT OF THE HONORABLE MARSHALL BILLINGSLEA, ASSISTANT SECRETARY, OFFICE OF TERRORISM AND FINANCIAL INTELLIGENCE, U.S. DEPARTMENT OF THE TREASURY

Mr. BILLINGSLEA. Chairman Royce, Ranking Member Engel, distinguished members of this committee, thank you for the opportunity to appear before you today to update you on the measures that the Treasury Department is undertaking in concert with the Department of State, and the broader administration efforts to deal with the unacceptable provocations and threats posed by North Korea.

In order to constrain Kim Jong Un, the international community has unanimously enacted multiple United Nations Security Council resolutions. In fact, with each provocation by North Korea's dictator, the nations of the world have responded with steadily tightening constraints of sanctions and embargoes.

Under previous administrations, the United Nations had already prohibited trade in matters such as arms, luxury goods, minerals, monuments, and the maintenance of offices and subsidiaries and bank accounts in North Korea. And while this had clearly inhibited North Korea's quest for weapons of mass destruction, it was not enough.

On August 5, our administration worked with the other permanent members of the U.N. Security Council to pass Resolution 2371, striking at the core of North Korea's revenue generation. That resolution, drafted by the United States, embargoes all importation of North Korean coal, iron, lead, and seafood now requires nations to cap employment of North Korean citizens sent abroad as slave labor.

Very importantly, last night, under Ambassador Haley's leadership, the United States passed, with the U.N. Security Council, Resolution 2375, which now targets North Korea's few remaining sources of revenue; very importantly, the export of textiles. It further restricts North Korea's ability to acquire revenue from overseas slave labor, and it cuts off about 55 percent of the refined petroleum products that are going into North Korea, and it bans further joint ventures with that regime.

These two recent resolutions are central to our efforts to mobilize the international community, and to deny funds to Kim Jong Un's weapons programs. The fact, however, is that North Korea has been living under U.N. sanctions for over a decade. It has nevertheless made significant strides toward its goal of building a nuclear-tipped ICBM. As is the case with any international agreement, the effectiveness of U.N. Security Council resolutions depends upon implementation and enforcement.

Kim Jong Un has two key financial vulnerabilities, which we are targeting in the Treasury Department: First, he needs revenue to maintain and expand his WMD and ballistic missile programs; and second, he needs access to the international and financial system to acquire the hard currency that Chairman Royce mentioned, to transfer funds, and to pay for goods, both licit and illicit.

There are only a number of finite ways that North Korea can raise significant amounts of foreign exchange, and for many years, coal has been the center of gravity for revenue generation. By our estimates, prior to the latest U.N. Security Council resolutions, coal shipments brought in more than $1 billion a year to the regime.

North Korea was making an additional $500 million or so from iron, lead, and seafood, and the textile ban will deny them around $800 million that they were generating in previous years. This is why these resolutions are so important. Again, effective implementation of this and all of the prior U.N. Security Council resolutions is essential.

Consistent with this, on August 22, we struck at the heart of North Korea's illegal coal trade with China. Treasury designated 16 individuals and entities, including three Chinese companies that are among the largest importers of North Korean coal. We estimate that collectively, these companies were responsible for importing nearly $½ billion worth of North Korean coal between 2013 and 2016. In doing this, we sent two clear messages: The first was to North Korea. We intend to deny the regime its last remaining sources of revenue unless and until it reverses course and denuclearizes.

The second message was to China, we are capable of tracking North Korea's trade in banned goods, such as coal, despite elaborate evasion schemes, and we will act even if the Chinese Government will not.

On June 1 of this year, we targeted a different kind of North Korean revenue, labor. We designated three individuals and six entities involved in that set of actions, and we also took actions in March. In total, under this administration, the Treasury Department is engaged in a full court press on Kim Jong Un's revenue generation networks, and we have singled out 37 specific entities involving the most lucrative types of trade.

Mr. Chairman, I want to share with you today another type of evasion scheme in which North Korea is engaged. As part of the efforts to acquire revenue, the regime employs deceptive shipping practices to conceal the true origin of goods. Pyongyang falsified the identity of vessels to make it harder for governments to determine if ships docking in their ports are linked to North Korea. And despite this evasion, we will expose the individuals and companies that are providing insurance, maintenance, or other services to North Korean vessels.

For instance, in June, we designated Dalian Global Unity, a Chinese company, that apparently was transferring about 700,000 tons of freight annually between China and North Korea. I am pleased to provide for the committee today, additional exposures of these duplicitous actions. The intelligence community has provided to your committee today evidence of how vessels originate in China, they turn off their transponders as they move into North Korean waters, they dock at North Korean ports, and they on-load commodities such as coal. They keep those transponders off, and then they turn them back on as they round to the South Korean peninsula, and they head into a Russian port.

In this particular case, this vessel, MV Bai Mei 8 registered from St. Kitts and Nevis, sat in that Russian port for a period of time, and then headed back out to water, ultimately docking back in China with North Korean origin coal. Sanctions evasion.

Of the second slide, which we will show now, is yet another example. In this particular example, you have a vessel that pulled
into North Korea, kept its transponder off, in violation of international maritime law, docked in Russia, offloaded the North Korean coal. Another vessel, that one was Panamanian, another vessel from Jamaica, the Jamaican flag, pulled in, picked up the North
Korean coal, and headed straight to China, again, to circumvent
U.N. sanctions.

Mr. Chairman, the other prong of our effort is to close in on the
way North Korea seeks to access the international financial system. Because of the sanctions regimes we have in place, it is difficult for North Korean individuals and entitles to do business in
their true names, and so that is why they maintain representatives
abroad who are engaged in all manner of obfuscation of creation of
shell and front companies—in fact, I dealt with many of these entities when I served in the private sector—to help conceal North Korea's overseas footprint.

These individuals are crucial to the North Korean regime because they have the expertise needed to establish front companies,
open bank accounts, and conduct transactions to move and launder
funds. It is incumbent upon the financial services industry, both
here and abroad, to stay vigilant, and I urge those who might be
implicated in the establishment of shell or front companies for the
DPRK, or anyone who is aware of such entitles, to come forward
with that information now, before they find themselves swept up
in our net.

We are closing in on North Korea's trade representatives. This
year we have already designated several bank and trading
operatives in China, Cuba, Russia, and Vietnam. And we are closely coordinating with the Department of Justice and others to target
these various North Korean networks that are transferring funds.

The chairman mentioned our actions with the Bank of Dandong.
We have designated that bank under Section 311 of the U.S.A. Patriot Act, and found it to be of a primary money laundering concern, and issued a notice for proposed rule making.

Again, I recognize that I am over time with the committee, therefore, I will wrap up my comments. But suffice to say, that our actions—this was the first Treasury Department action in over a decade that targeted a non-North Korean bank for facilitating North
Korean financial activity. It demonstrates our commitment to take
action. We look forward to taking action with the Chinese where
possible. And in the event that that is not possible, we will, nevertheless, move forward to safeguard the U.S. and international financial system. Thank you, Chairman.

[The prepared statement of Mr. Billingslea follows:]

Testimony of Assistant Secretary Marshall S. Billingslea
House Foreign Affairs Committee
Tuesday, September 12, 2017

Chairman Royce, Ranking Member Engel, and distinguished members of this Committee, thank you for the opportunity to update the Committee on the Treasury Department's efforts to counter the urgent threat posed by North Korea.

This is my first time testifying as Treasury's Assistant Secretary for Terrorist Financing. I am honored to represent the Department today. Under the leadership of Secretary Mnuchin and Under Secretary Mandelker, Treasury has developed and is actively implementing a campaign designed to impose maximum pressure on North Korea's finances and economy. We are working as part of the Administration's overall effort to eliminate the danger posed to the United States and our allies by Kim Jong-Un's nuclear and ballistic missile programs. I am here today to publicly share aspects of the plan, assess our progress thus far and describe the challenges we face.

The Threat Posed by North Korea

North Korea poses a grave and growing threat to the security of the United States, our friends and allies in Asia, and – indeed – the world as a whole. Kim Jong-Un has dramatically increased the pace of ballistic missile testing since coming to power. This year alone, North Korea has conducted sixteen missile tests, including two intercontinental ballistic missile (ICBM) tests. Just a few days ago, on August 28, North Korea launched a missile directly over Japan. Not only was this a violation of United Nations Security Council resolutions, it imperiled Japanese airspace and clearly was meant as a blatant threat to the people of Japan, and to us and our armed forces stationed there. North Korea's latest test of a nuclear device, conducted over the Labor Day weekend, marks an unacceptable provocation.

Kim Jong-Un has issued multiple threats to target American cities and territories. His recent pronouncements regarding the conduct of salvo missile launches at Guam are just one example. We take these threats with the utmost seriousness, and are determined to constrain Kim Jong-Un's capacity to act on such threats in the future. We will not allow North Korea to extort and threaten the world with its nuclear and missile programs.

In order to constrain Kim Jong-Un, the international community has unanimously enacted multiple United Nations Security Council resolutions. In fact, with each provocation by North Korea's dictator, the nations of the world have responded with steadily tightening constraints of sanctions and embargoes.

Under previous Administrations, the UN had prohibited trade in arms, luxury goods, minerals, monuments, and the maintenance of representative offices, subsidiaries or bank accounts in North Korea. While this clearly had inhibited North Korea's quest for weapons of mass destruction (WMD), it was not enough. On August 5, our Administration worked with the other Permanent Members of the Security Council to pass UN Security Council Resolutions 2371, striking at the core of North Korea's revenue generation. That resolution, drafted by the United

States, embargoes all importation of North Korean coal, iron, lead and seafood and now requires nations to cap employment of North Korean citizens sent abroad as workers. Very importantly, last night, on September 11, the UN passed resolution 2375, targeting North Korea's ability to export textiles, further restricting North Korea's ability to acquire revenue from overseas laborers, cutting off over 55 percent of refined petroleum products going to North Korea, and fully banning all joint ventures with North Korea to cut off foreign investments. These two recent resolutions are central to our efforts to mobilize the international community and to deny funds to Kim Jong-Un's weapons programs.

The fact is, however, that North Korea has been living under UN sanctions for over a decade, and nevertheless has made significant progress toward its goal of building a nuclear-tipped ICBM. As is the case with any international agreement, the key to effectiveness of UN Security Council resolutions is *implementation.*

All nations must join us in implementing all relevant United Nations Security Council resolutions, including the most recently enacted ones. North Korea continues to defy the UN arms embargo and is continually engaged in efforts to evade the sanctions and prohibitions adopted in nine separate UN Security Council resolutions. As both the UN and the U.S. sanctions regimes expand in response to Kim Jong-Un's reckless behavior, so too does the depth and breadth of North Korea's sanctions evasion efforts. Because of uneven, and sometimes nonexistent, international implementation, North Korea shrugs off the practical impact of many restrictions, and is still exporting prohibited goods such as weapons, minerals, and statues.

North Korea's leadership also continues to smuggle in luxury goods while neglecting the urgent, basic needs of its citizens. The humanitarian suffering of the North Korean people stands in stark contrast to the opulent lifestyle of Kim Jong-Un and North Korea's senior leaders. To finance their excesses, as well as the nuclear and ballistic missile programs, the regime is evading financial restrictions by using overseas financial representatives and a web of front and shell companies. North Korea has proven adept at using the interconnected global financial system to its advantage and employing deceptive financial practices to cover its tracks. North Korea is at times very sophisticated in how it sets up financial intermediaries. But in some countries where the will to fully implement and enforce sanctions has been lacking, North Korea can often be brazen in how it accesses financial networks.

Using all the information available to the U.S. government, the Treasury Department is mapping out North Korea's financial and revenue-generating mechanisms.

Applying Maximum Economic Pressure on North Korea

Kim Jong-Un has two key financial vulnerabilities. First, he needs revenue to maintain and expand his WMD and ballistic missile programs. Second, he needs access to the international financial system to acquire hard currency, transfer funds, and pay for goods for both licit and illicit purposes. We are therefore actively working to cut off Kim Jong-Un's ability to both raise and move money through the international financial system.

<u>Targeting DPRK Revenue</u>

There are only a finite number of ways that North Korea can raise significant amounts of foreign exchange. For many years, coal has been the center of gravity for North Korea's revenue generation. By our estimates, prior to the latest UN Security Council resolutions, coal shipments brought in $1 billion in revenue annually for the regime. Prior to the latest UNSCR, North Korea made another estimated $500 million annually from iron, lead, and seafood. In the past, an important source of funding was the export of weapons and missile technology, but now North Korea acquires revenue from exporting commodities. That is why the August 5 UN Security Council Resolution 2371 is so important. It prohibits UN Member States from importing any of these items from North Korea.

But, as I noted, effective implementation of all UNSCRs is essential if we are to deny North Korea its current, principal sources of funds. Treasury, in coordination with the State Department, is working to accomplish just that. We do this in a number of ways. With friends and allies, we share detailed information regarding North Korean activities to assist them in disrupting sanctions evasion and illicit trade. The Treasury Department routinely engages at multiple levels with partner nations to help them conduct detailed forensic investigation and analysis to target North Korean financial networks where they exist.

For instance, on August 22, we struck at the heart of North Korea's illegal coal trade with China. Treasury designated 16 individuals and entities, including three Chinese companies that are among the largest importers of North Korean coal. We estimate that collectively these companies were responsible for importing nearly half a billion dollars' worth of North Korean coal between 2013 and 2016. These funds are used to support the Government of North Korea and the Workers' Party of Korea, including its nuclear and ballistic missile programs. On top of that, we know that some of these companies were also buying luxury items and sending an array of products back to the North Korean regime. On August 22 we sent two clear messages. The first was to North Korea: we intend to deny the regime its last remaining sources of revenue, unless and until it reverses course and denuclearizes. The second message was to China. We are capable of tracking North Korea's trade in banned goods, such as coal, despite elaborate evasion schemes, and we will act even if the Chinese government will not.

Importantly, our August actions were matched by swift legally-binding domestic designations in Japan, and by a public advisory from South Korea's Ministry of Strategy and Finance cautioning all South Korean nationals from conducting financial transactions with these U.S. designated individuals and entities. It strongly advised that South Korean nationals exercise particular caution against transactions with the designated individuals and entities. Our disruption efforts against North Korean networks are maximized when nations act forcefully, in concert. We appreciate the steps taken by Japan and South Korea, and we look to other friendly and allied nations in the region to do the same.

I also note, for the Committee, that our August actions followed two earlier rounds of domestic sanctions. On June 1 of this year, the Administration targeted a different type of North Korean revenue: labor. We designated three individuals and six entities, including the Korea Computer Center (KCC), a state-run IT research and development center that was operating in Germany, China, Syria, India, and the Middle East. Using overseas North Korean laborers, KCC was earning foreign currency for North Korea's Munitions Industry Department, which is responsible for overseeing the ballistic missile program. In addition to these sanctions, behind the scenes, both we and the State Department have aggressively engaged dozens of countries where North Korean workers were employed, often by so-called construction companies. I am pleased that in many cases, our efforts have led to the scaling back or outright expulsion of these workers – yet another financial blow to the regime.

Finally, recall that on March 1, Treasury designated twelve individuals and entities, including North Korea-based Paeksol Trading Corporation, which was selling coal and iron ore to China. The revenue from these sales supported the UN- and U.S.-designated Reconnaissance General Bureau, North Korea's premiere intelligence organization that is also involved in the government's conventional arms trade.

In total, under this Administration, the Treasury Department is engaged in a full court press on Kim Jong-Un's revenue generation networks. We have singled out 37 specific entities involved in the most lucrative types of trade remaining to the regime, such as coal, iron, and labor. These are just the companies and people that we have decided to designate publicly. As noted, other parts of the network we have chosen to disrupt through non-public measures, working with friends and allies. North Korea will certainly continue to morph its procurement and sales networks in response to our actions, and we will be relentless in our pursuit.

<u>Shipping</u>

As part of North Korea's efforts to acquire revenue, the regime uses shipping networks to import and export goods. North Korea employs deceptive practices to conceal the true origin of these goods. Pyongyang has been found to routinely falsify a vessel's identity and documentation, complicating the ability of governments to determine if a vessel docking in their ports is linked to North Korea. We are actively increasing our understanding of North Korea's shipping networks, and we will expose individuals and companies that are providing insurance, maintenance, or other services to North Korean vessels. In June, the Treasury Department designated Dalian Global Unity, a Chinese company that was reported to transport 700,000 tons of freight annually between China and North Korea. Dalian Global Unity was also involved in smuggling luxury goods, with middlemen from the company giving specific instructions about how to evade the UN-mandated luxury goods ban. The Treasury Department has extensive experience mapping and dismantling illicit shipping networks, having worked for many years to uncover deceptive Iranian shipping practices. We are applying lessons learned in the Iran context to target commercial shipping moving in and out of North Korea.

Accordingly, I am pleased to offer for the Committee's consideration today several images, provided by the Intelligence Community, which clearly shows deceptive shipping practices used by the North Koreans. In the following images, you see examples that demonstrate that North Korea is using deceptive practices to mask the origin of exported coal to Russia and China. In the first example, the ship travels from China and declares that it is travelling to Russia. During its journey, the ship turns off its automatic identification system (AIS), probably stops in North Korea to load coal, travels to Vladivostok, Russia, and then returns to China probably to offload the coal.

We are making this information available today to the Committee and to the public, and are also sharing with other nations as we take steps to curtail these deceptive practices and enforce the UN embargoes on coal, iron and iron ore, and other commodities.

<u>Preventing Access to the Global Financial System</u>

North Korea also uses deceptive practices to access the global financial system. As we constrain North Korea's ability to generate revenue, we continue to disrupt the regime's attempts to access the U.S. and international financial systems. North Korea seeks to use the funds it earns abroad to pay its bills and purchase goods. Because of the robust international sanctions regime in place, it is difficult for North Korean individuals and entities to do business in their true names. So in order to access the international financial system, North Korea maintains representatives abroad who work on behalf of UN- and U.S.-designated North Korean banks and trading companies, helping North Korea conceal their overseas footprint.

These individuals are important to North Korean networks because they have expertise that they use to establish front companies, open bank accounts, and conduct transactions enabling North Korea to launder funds. Without them, Kim Jong-Un's regime will find it much harder to develop the layers of obfuscation necessary to evade our steadily constricting campaign. We urge the private sector, particularly in Asian financial hubs, to stay vigilant. North Korean financial facilitators are violating both international and U.S. law. Those who collaborate with them are exposing themselves to enormous jeopardy. So too are the bankers, accountants, tax advisors, and notaries who participate in North Korean deception. It is incumbent on those in the financial services industry who might be implicated in the establishment of shell or front companies for the DPRK, and anyone who is aware of such entities, to come forward with that information now, before they find themselves swept up in our net.

We are committed to stopping this activity wherever it occurs. Treasury is working with foreign governments, U.S. law enforcement, and the private sector to expose North Korea's deceptive practices, prevent them from conducting international transactions, and freeze these funds.

This year, Treasury designated North Korean bank and trading representatives who were operating in China, Cuba, Russia, and Vietnam. These designations prohibited these individuals from accessing the U.S. financial system, alerted banks to the risk they posed, and pressured governments harboring these facilitators to abide by their UN Security Council obligations, expel these representatives, and freeze their assets. We expect more actions to come.

North Korea's illicit financial activity is not just conducted in dollars. Nor is it limited to a handful of legal jurisdictions. We also are concerned about North Korea's use of euros and other currencies. Once a North Korean trade representative successfully places revenue into a nation's financial system, that revenue often then flows indirectly through global banks, who are unwittingly conducting currency clearing operations for North Korean front companies. Obviously, financial institutions conducting transactions or clearing funds for North Korean front companies are likely violating UN sanctions. The challenge, however, is how to identify the North Korean front companies in the first place. Treasury is working with governments around the world, particularly those with banks engaged in euro-clearing, to share typologies of North

Korean sanctions evasion. This includes the sharing of specific information with Ministries of Finance, Central Banks, and Financial Intelligence Units to assist in protecting their currency clearing processes from abuse by North Korea.

Similarly, Treasury is also closely coordinating with the Department of Justice to target North Korean networks transferring money through the U.S. financial system. In June and August, Treasury designated a Russian network selling petroleum to North Korea. The Independent Petroleum Company (IPC), a Russian company, has reportedly shipped over $1 million worth of petroleum products to North Korea. In order to pay for the petroleum, North Korea set up front companies that could transfer funds on behalf of the UN- and U.S.-designated Foreign Trade Bank. Treasury designated the three individuals and two front companies involved in the scheme and froze the funds moving through the U.S. financial system. On the same day, the Department of Justice issued a civil forfeiture complaint against the companies to seize almost $7 million held by U.S. banks, belonging to those entities and individuals.

Similarly, on June 29, Treasury took action against a Chinese bank: Bank of Dandong. Pursuant to Section 311 of the USA PATRIOT Act, Treasury found the bank to be of "primary money laundering concern" and issued a notice of proposed rulemaking, which, if finalized, would essentially cut Bank of Dandong off from the U.S. financial system. Among other things, Bank of Dandong is believed to act as a financial conduit for North Korea to access the U.S. and international financial systems, including by facilitating millions of dollars of transactions for companies involved in North Korea's WMD and ballistic missile programs.

This was the Treasury Department's first action in over a decade that targeted a non-North Korean bank for facilitating North Korean financial activity. It clearly demonstrates the Administration's commitment to protecting the integrity of both the U.S. and international financial systems. Financial institutions in China, or elsewhere, that continue to process transactions on behalf of North Korea should take heed. We will continue to target North Korea's illicit activity, regardless of location.

<u>Challenges and Opportunities</u>

It is essential that the international community work together to increase economic pressure on North Korea. North Korea is a threat to global peace and security. Moreover, Kim Jong-Un's regime operates globally, and therefore we need global cooperation to constrain its finances. All UN Member States must, at minimum, implement and enforce UN Security Council Resolutions, which are binding.

But we can, and should, do more. We are working bilaterally with key partners to coordinate our domestic sanctions programs. We are pleased that, this year, Australia expanded its sanctions programs to target additional sectors of the North Korean economy, and that Japan and South Korea – as I noted – have issued domestic actions targeting North Korea. Under Secretary Mandelker is currently in Europe discussing our work with our European allies to increase sanctions and combat North Korea's sanctions evasion, and Treasury's leadership is engaged with leaders from Southeast Asia and Africa on the importance of implementing UNSCRs. We are also working bilaterally with governments and through the Financial Action Task Force to ensure that countries have the regulatory framework in place to detect and freeze assets linked to North Korea.

But challenges remain. Certainly China and Russia are to be recognized for supporting adoption of the most recent Security Council Resolution. Nevertheless, both countries must do much more to implement and enforce the sanctions called for by the United Nations. Russian companies continue to provide support to North Korea. DPRK bank representatives operate in Russia in flagrant disregard of the very resolutions adopted by Russia at the UN. This summer, for instance, Treasury designated Russian companies Gefest and Ardis Bearings, as well as their directors, for providing support directly to North Korean entities involved in WMD and ballistic missile procurement. This activity is unacceptable, and we will continue to target those entities and individuals anywhere, including Russia, who provide any support to North Korea's procurement networks.

China is even more central to a successful resolution of the crisis caused by Kim Jong-Un. China accounts for at least 90 percent of North Korea's exports. North Korea is overwhelmingly dependent upon China for both trade and access to the international financial system. China's full and effective enforcement of UN sanctions is therefore essential. Unfortunately, I cannot assure the Committee today that we have seen sufficient evidence of China's willingness to truly shut down North Korean revenue flows, expunge the North Korean illicit actors from its banking system, and expel the North Korean middlemen and brokers who are establishing webs of front companies. We will continue to work with the Chinese to maximize economic pressure on North Korea, but we will not hesitate to act unilaterally. If China wishes to avoid future measures, such as those imposed on Bank of Dandong or the various companies sanctioned for illegal trade practices, then it urgently needs to take demonstrable public steps to eliminate North Korea's trade and financial access.

Conclusion

Mr. Chairman, Ranking Member Engel, and Members of the Committee: I reiterate my appreciation for the opportunity to testify before you today on this administration's efforts to combat the threat posed by North Korea's deadly weapons programs. Treasury is engaged on a daily basis in "hand-to-hand" financial combat with North Korea's illicit networks. We do this with the full recognition that our success in curtailing North Korea's revenue streams and shutting off its access to financial systems is essential to a peaceful resolution of the growing crisis. As I have indicated, we will target North Korea's economic activities and sanctions evasion schemes regardless of where they occur. We are approaching the problem strategically, but given the urgency of the threat, we will continue to apply maximum pressure on North Korea, and on those countries where the DPRK operates, at every turn.

Thank you and I look forward to your questions.

Chairman ROYCE. Assistant Secretary Billingslea, thank you very much. Let me make a point in terms of when we have seen sanctions that were effective. In 2005, we had the sanctions on Banco Delta Asia. At that point in time, in talking to a senior defector that worked in their missile program, he indicated that because we had cut off the hard currency, they had to shut down their ICBM program.

One of the things he indicated also, or was indicated by the conversations we had with senior defectors, was that during that period of time, the ability of the regime, or the dictator as they called him, to get his hands on hard currency, was blocked. And the inability of a dictator to be able to pay his generals—and this was the quote—"is a very bad position for a dictator to be in."

In retrospect, we, therefore, say two things happen during that period of time in terms of the desperation of the situation within the Kim regime. This was under his father, Kim Jong Il. We have the ability to replicate that if we have the will to do what was done in 2005. And in 2005, it was maybe a dozen banks that were being used. At that time, Treasury found that North Korea was counterfeiting $100 U.S. bills, and that gave Treasury the authority to do this until such time as the Department of State forced them to lift the asset freezes.

But during that time, we had an enormous amount of pressure being brought to bear. In this particular case—and let me use your words here—but it is China that is primarily involved in the support system in terms of, I would estimate, 90 percent of the hard currency that the regime needs. Now, we have managed to cut off a lot of that because it is very expensive to run an ICBM program, or a nuclear weapons program, billions and billions and billions of dollars. North Korea's money has no value, so they have to get this foreign currency into the country in order to pay for it on a month to month basis, in terms of what they are trying to build out.

You said if China wishes to avoid future measures such as those imposed on Bank of Dandong, or the various companies sanctioned for illegal trade practices, then it urgently needs to take demonstrable public steps to eliminate North Korea's trade and financial access. That is the point to us here in Congress. Some of our opinion on this, in terms of Congress, is affected by the fact that China's biggest banks, even state-owned banks, still do business with North Korea. That has got to end completely. We cannot accept half measures on this. These transactions are what supports the regime's nuclear program.

And I understand the administration is pressing Beijing to take action here. I understand that many of these banks have significant operations in the United States, and that there would be consequences to our economy. However, U.S. presence is the very thing that makes our sanctions so powerful. They would rather do business with us than North Korea in terms of how consequential that is to these institutions.

So at what point do we designate these major Chinese banks for doing business with North Korea? We have done our outreach to Beijing, with limited results. Shouldn't we demonstrate the seriousness with which we take the North Korean nuclear threat, while further isolating that regime in North Korea, Kim Jong Un, from the financial system that he uses to build out his atomic weapons program?

Mr. BILLINGSLEA. Chairman, first, let me say that China and Russia are to be recognized for supporting the adoption of the two most recent U.N. Security Council resolutions, which are significant for the clamp-down that they enable us to place on Kim Jong Un's revenue. However, we have been very clear that if China wishes to avoid further measures, such as that which happened to the Bank of Dandong, we urgently need to see demonstrable action.

I cannot tell the committee today that we have seen sufficient evidence of China's willingness to truly shut down North Korean revenue flows, to expunge North Korean illicit actors from its banking system, or to expel the various North Korean middlemen and brokers who are continuing to establish webs of front companies. We need to see that happen.

Chairman ROYCE. To both our Assistant Secretaries, let me say this: Last night we saw the Security Council unanimously approve its third U.N. sanctions resolution this year on North Korea. And this latest measure restricts the regime's oil imports while banning textile exports in joint ventures. However, the nature of the Security Council means that this was a compromise to ensure the regime cannot claim this compromise that came out of this was a victory, which is what they will try to do. We have got to demonstrate the impact of these new international sanctions by making certain that this time, no one is skirting those sanctions.

So what steps will the Departments of State and Treasury take in the coming days to implement the new Security Council resolution? And how will these actions that you are about to take, send this clear message to Kim Jong Un on the reality that this time, we are going to follow through with enforcement and give them no space in terms of additional hard currency?

Ms. THORNTON. Thank you, Mr. Chairman. It is very clear in the process of ramping up this peaceful pressure campaign on the North Korean regime, that one of the key elements is to keep to global coalition that we have got behind these sanctions together, and to keep every single country in the coalition working actively to continue to squeeze on trade, on labors, on financial transactions, on shipping, et cetera. And what we have been doing in the Department of State is working across the board with every one of our diplomatic partners around the world. The Secretary raises the North Korea issue in every single one of his meetings with foreign leaders. And we have seen a great response from countries around the world who are increasingly outraged over North Korea's provocative behavior.

So we have really been working hard to close the net. We have seen diplomatic establishments closed, ambassadors kicked out, other North Korean representatives kicked out. The Philippines announced recently they are going to cut complete trade with North Korea. So we are having an effect on a lot of the networks that the North Koreans have built around the world.

I think the sanctions, 2371, last month, and now, 2375, last night, we are going to be working aggressively to make sure that we and all of our partners around the world, too, are working with every country that we can to make sure that every country has the capacity to track illicit transactions, to go after violators, and raising consciousness, but, also, giving them the tools to go after those bad actors, is what we are focused on.

We are trying to clean up ship registries and give countries the ability to better track the shipping of ships that are flagged under their flag, et cetera. So I think we are still working on implementing these most recent two U.N. Security Council resolutions. We also have an ongoing, very close dialogue with the Chinese on what they are doing to track sanctions, and we share a lot of information with them, but we will also drive them to shut down networks that we find.

Chairman ROYCE. Thank you, Assistant Secretary Thornton, my time has expired. I am going to go to Mr. Engel for his questions.

Mr. ENGEL. Thank you, Mr. Chairman. You know, when I was in North Korea, and this is a while back, but twice, one of the things that struck me, we had just deposed Saddam Hussein, and one of the top North Korean officials—it wasn't the leader, but it was a very high ranking official—said to us, Saddam Hussein didn't have nuclear weapons, and look where he is now. From those two trips I took, that is the one thing that rang in my ears. And now, of course, they are carrying out those horrific words.

Secretary Thornton, let me ask you, in Europe we have NATO. Obviously, in Asia, we don't have a treaty group like NATO. So how do we reassure, in your view, our allies who doubt our resolve to defend Tokyo or Seoul, because we are afraid of what might happen in Los Angeles or Guam or any other place? How do we reassure our allies?

Ms. THORNTON. Yes, thank you, Ranking Member. I think we have been working very, very closely with both South Korea and Japan, but also with all the other counties in the Asia-Pacific region on confronting the North Korea challenge. Obviously, we have a very close and continuing conversation with both Japan and Korea, not just the State Department, but the Department of Defense, on managing our alliances. Obviously, we have been talking to both Japan and Korea, as the chairman mentioned, about additional defensive needs and capabilities that they may have, that they want to move ahead on. And so, I think the reassurance that we have been providing them with, and the constant close communication with them, and with others in the region, has been of significant reassurance to them about our ongoing commitment to defense of our allies.

Mr. ENGEL. Thank you very much. Secretary Billingslea, could you identify the top, say, 25 firms that compose North Koreans illicit network? And if so, would you be willing to provide that information to this committee in classified form, if necessary?

Mr. BILLINGSLEA. Ranking Member, yes. We would be pleased to have a classified discussion with you on a number of North Korean entities that we are actively targeting. However, once we choose to move with designations and blocking of assets and so forth, we would want to keep that kind of information very close hold until we are ready to move so that the money doesn't flee in advance of our actions.

Mr. ENGEL. Okay. I think it would be interesting in this committee for such a gathering, so we will be in touch with you. We will do it together, the chairman and I.

Let me ask you about these entities. If Beijing and the other relevant governments haven't taken sufficient action to close these entities and curb their activities, have we taken action to designate these entities under U.S. law?

Mr. BILLINGSLEA. Yes, sir, we have. We have done a couple of waves of that under this administration. Our August 22 actions that I referenced were probably the most noteworthy, and are definitely a signal of things to come.

Mr. ENGEL. It is my understanding that these entities operate in China in a small number of the jurisdictions. Have we informed Beijing of the activities of these entities and communicated the expectation of the U.S. Government that their actions be curbed?

Mr. BILLINGSLEA. Yes, sir. Both the Department of the Treasury and the Department of State are in repeated communications with our counterparts in China, often very specifically with respect to entities that we believe are associated with the North Korean regime, and we make very specific requests for action on these entities.

Mr. ENGEL. Thank you. Look, this is a problem that goes back to a number of administrations before this one, and the President did inherit a complex and intractable foreign policy in North Korea, but his mixed and inconsistent messaging is self-inflicted—it is a self-inflicted wound. Again, I don't see the purpose of arguing with South Korea on trade at a time when we need to show strong and resolve.

So let me ask you this: I have so many questions to ask, I never can get them in in a short period of time. But let me go back to you, Secretary Billingslea, the chairman mentioned several large Chinese banks in his remarks. China Merchants Bank was one of them. Have we taken action against them, and if we haven't, why haven't we?

Mr. BILLINGSLEA. So, Congressman, we have taken action against Bank of Dandong, as was discussed earlier, which we believe is a money laundering concern associated with North Korea. And our actions have had a very clear effect on that bank's operations. That is a signal of our intent to move forward with expunging from the international financial system any financial institution which is taking insufficient action from an anti-money laundering standpoint against North Korea.

We believe that the next most important thing to do here is to, very specifically, target and expose those individuals who are the financial facilitators for the North Korean regime who set up these elaborate front and shell company structures, which are then used to get the bank accounts to launder the money. That is a priority focus area for us, and we are driving very quickly forward on that matter.

Mr. ENGEL. Thank you. Secretary Thornton, did you want to add something to——

Ms. THORNTON. Yeah. I just wanted to note for the committee that the Chinese have announced in the last couple of days, measures against all of their big banks operating, particularly in north-east China, issuing warnings and prohibitions about opening accounts for North Korean actors. So they are actually feeling some pressure on this and making public statements.

Mr. ENGEL. One quick thing. You both would agree that any kind of resolution or partial restitution of this crisis has to go through China, that it is virtually impossible to not involve China. China, I think we all think is the one country that can influence North Korean behavior. Do you both agree with that?

Mr. BILLINGSLEA. I do.

Mr. ENGEL. Okay. Thank you. Thank you, Mr. Chairman.

Chairman ROYCE. Thank you, Mr. Engel. We go now to Mr. Chris Smith of New Jersey, whose subcommittee leads our work on human rights.

Mr. SMITH. Thank you very much, Mr. Chairman, for your leadership, and for putting together this important hearing. And I do want to thank our distinguished witnesses for painstakingly working the details of this. It is an extremely difficult fight, and I want to thank you for what you are doing every day to make a difference.

I also want to express my deepest respect to Ambassador Haley and the administration for drafting Resolution 2375. As you have pointed out, the toughest sanctions ever meted out against North Korea. My hope is that China and Russia will comply with the terms and conditions, and you might want to speak to your expectations about that, because obviously in the past, it has been lackluster in many ways.

I would also appreciate your thoughts on how you judge the success or failure of strategic patience, and whether or not you thought that aided and got us to where we are at now, or was this inevitable anyway? For many, there is a significant, and I think a profoundly significant, under-appreciation for Juche, the dictatorship cult, deification of Kim Il-sung. I read books about it. I have talked to many of the diaspora and refugees who speak, and they say: "You Americans don't get it." The worship of Kim Il-sung is so profound, so deeply embedded, and it does lead to a fanaticism that rivals ISIS-like fanaticism about what they would do for their leader, the great leader, going back, and now the current leader.

Do you think an information surge—there is nothing that precludes us from broadcasting, despite jamming capabilities that they might have. Can de-mythify the Kims because the big lie has certainly been imbedded in the hearts and minds of so many North Koreans for so long?

Every time I talk to a group of defectors, and I ask them that question, they explain eloquently about how from the youngest age right up—and those expressions when one of the leaders die, and the tears and people throwing themselves on the ground, it is not fake. It is fanaticism. And when it comes to the military, that means that that fanaticism will be carried out with horrific consequences for those that are defending liberty in South Korea and elsewhere.

Finally, we know that China subsidizes North Korea's bad behavior. It enables torture of asylum seekers by repatriating those who escape to China, in direct contravention of the refugee convention, and provides Kim Jong Un needed currency by employing thousands of trafficked workers. And I am wondering if the Department is looking at, with regards to China, imposing Magnitsky-like sanctions against those who are complicit in those crimes?

Even the U.N. Commission on Inquiry for North Korea recommended that sanctions be used to target individuals. We have got the law. And I hope that is something that is under active consideration, and hopefully we will hear soon about individuals being so targeted. Ms. Thornton.

Ms. THORNTON. Yeah, thank you very much. I think, you know, of course, the U.S. State Department has been very concerned about the egregious human rights situation in North Korea for decades. We have had a special representative working on these issues. We have worked very closely with him. I think we have made some good progress, or at least we have taken a number of very significant actions in this area, and will continue to do so.

I think the question of increasing information access inside North Korea is one that we certainly have looked at and are working on, and whether we can do more there, I think we are always looking at whether we can do more and what we can do more effectively. But I think, from my standpoint, one of the biggest ways we can get people inside North Korea to question what the regime is doing is by making it very difficult for them to pay the military and to provide for their citizens, and I think that is really what we are very focused on, in addition to trying to knock down the proliferation networks that are contributing to the weapons program. So there is a litany of egregious behavior across the board, and we want to go after every single aspect of that. But I think looking at cutting off the economic flows to North Korea is another way of——

Mr. SMITH. Of course, that would include the complicity of Iran with the ballistic missile program in North Korea?

Ms. THORNTON. Sorry, I didn't get the connection.

Mr. SMITH. The cooperation between the Iranians and Pyongyang when it comes to ballistic missiles, that was something that I and others asked when the Iran deal was being contemplated. And, unfortunately, that was left off the table in the final agreement, that the concern is that that cooperation continues today, and I hope that that is something that is very aggressively being pursued as well.

Ms. THORNTON. Yeah. We are certainly looking at that.

Mr. BILLINGSLEA. Yes, sir.

Mr. SMITH. But you didn't want to speak to Juche?

Mr. BILLINGSLEA. Well, first of all, Congressman, your leadership on human rights matters has been—for quite a long time. I had a chance to work for you when I was a staffer on the Senate Foreign Relations Committee back in the 1990s under Chairman Helms in those days. Again, I appreciate the stand that you take on these matters.

We are very specifically looking at a number of individuals in North Korea who are engaged in egregious, outrageous human rights abuses. This matter of Juche, I think you have articulated it exactly correctly. However, I am not sure that the cult personality necessarily extends to all of the elites right around the dear leader. He very much depends upon this hard currency revenue, as the chairman noted, to maintain his opulent lifestyle and the people around him. And so the extent to which draining his ability to generate hard currency not only constricts his ability to engage in WMD and missile programs, but it also presumably increases the fragility of the regime around him. This is, as we would say, a twofer in our view.

Chairman ROYCE. Mr. Brad Sherman of California.

Mr. SHERMAN. Soon, North Korea will have more nuclear weapons than they feel is absolutely necessarily to defend themselves from us. But they will need hard currency. They might prefer actual cash currency. Iran is having some constraints on its ability to develop nuclear weapons. Mr. Secretary, do we have any understanding with China that nonstop flights between Pyongyang and Tehran will be forced to stop for fueling, or do we have anything else that would prevent this obvious economic deal?

Mr. BILLINGSLEA. I will defer to the State Department on the specific discussions on Air Koryo and flights in——

Mr. SHERMAN. Right.

Mr. BILLINGSLEA [continuing]. And from North Korea. I would also, Congressman, note that, as we move forward on these two successive——

Mr. SHERMAN. I am not asking—I have very limited time. Do we have anything or not?

Ms. THORNTON. I know that we have limitations on air refueling. I know the Chinese have refused to refuel. So there is pressure on——

Mr. SHERMAN. No, I am not asking—I am saying, do we have any understanding with China that there will be nonstop, no refueling planes going from Tehran to Pyongyang loaded with currency or coming back with a nuclear weapon?

Ms. THORNTON. No, we don't.

Mr. SHERMAN. We don't. Okay.

Ms. THORNTON. A nonstop plane from——

Mr. SHERMAN. So we have one country that has over $1 billion in Saran wrapped hard currency. And we have another country that, if the Assistant Secretary's work is done well, will need $1 billion in currency and will have quite a number of nuclear weapons that they could sell.

Folks, I have been coming to this room for 20 years, and not much has changed. We have Ileana smiling down upon us; that is good. We got some electronics. But for 20 years, administrations have been coming here and telling me that we don't have to make any concessions to North Korea, we don't have to do anything that would make any single American company upset, and we are going to make the American people safe. And for 20 years, I have been hearing that over and over again. I hear that we are going to have unprecedented sanctions, which means that we found a few more companies to sanction, just as they have invented a few more companies and created them. Whether we can list them faster than they can create them, I don't know. But the fact is that North Korea's real GDP has grown 50 percent in the last 20 years.

Assistant Secretary, if you were successful with your sanctions, you might just cause them not to increase their GDP, which means they still have 50 percent more than they found necessary to hold on to power back in 1997. But while we haven't made the American people safer, we have met the political objectives here in the United States. We don't threaten China, even a little bit, with country sanctions, because that would be politically difficult for the United States to do. We don't adopt reasonable objectives, like a freeze in the North Korean program, because that would be politically difficult to do.

What we do is what we have been doing—for 20 years, and then Chairman Royce has always come up with this or that better sanction. Sometimes his ideas are listened to; sometimes they are not. But there is never enough pressure on the North Korean regime to cause regime-threatening levels. This is a regime that survived the famines in the 1990s, late 1990s. Now their GDP is higher than it has been—it has gone up just about every year. And China is not going to allow us to put regime-threatening pressure on the North Korean regime. They may, you know, punish them a little bit for what they are doing and how they are doing it and how disruptive they are and how headline-grabbing they are.

But, Mr. Assistant Secretary, do we even have a plan for threatening China with country sanctions, tariffs on all goods? Or is it just a matter that, "Well, your number seven bank won't be able to do business in the United States, so your number eight bank and numbers one through five banks will"? If you were running a retailer, would you think there was the slightest risk of your supply chain to China because of China's unwillingness to engage in the kinds of sanctions necessary just to get a freeze of the nuclear program?

Mr. BILLINGSLEA. Congressman, I think you raise a good point. And the chairman noted that China is central to this matter. Ninety percent of North Korean——

Mr. SHERMAN. And we are not doing enough to force them to change their behavior, which is to punish North Korea a little bit for being a little bit too flamboyant in their actions but to make sure that the regime can survive. And this regime won't even agree to a freeze of their nuclear program unless you have something relatively, at least halfway, toward regime-threatening sanctions.

Mr. BILLINGSLEA. Yeah, I am not sure I agree with that. We are——

Mr. SHERMAN. You think the regime would give up its nuclear program, even if they said, well, we can survive these sanctions, but we care so much about our people that we are going to—we care about our GDP, we might——

Mr. BILLINGSLEA. No, I wouldn't speculate on regime thought processes. What I would focus on is the Chinese as the center of gravity here. And I think that—in fact, I know that, from a tempo standpoint and from a pressure standpoint, the pace of action that we have taken, even on my——

Mr. SHERMAN. It is unprecedented, just like the last 19 years people have sat in that chair and told me it is unprecedented. But it has certainly not been enough stop——

Chairman ROYCE. Will the gentleman yield?

Mr. SHERMAN. I will yield.

Chairman ROYCE. I think the gentleman is raising exactly the bottom-line question here. In other words, we are deferential here to a point, but it has been a long time since the 1994 framework agreement with North Korea. It has been a long, long time of waiting for China to comply with the sanctions we pass and, frankly, with the sanctions that the United Nations pass.

As you have just laid out for us with the charts that you provided, China understands that that coal is coming, circumventing the sanctions, and being unloaded, just as they understand that these banks are not complying with the provisions that have been passed by the Security Council.

I think that Mr. Sherman raises a point. I have only seen once, in 2005, in response, as I said, to North Korea counterfeiting our currency—and that power was soon taken away from the Treasury—that I ever saw anything that cut off hard currency into the regime. And that was because we didn't give anyone an option, anywhere. If you were doing business, we were shutting down those institutions.

So I would just say this is where the discussion needs to go next if there isn't full compliance with the sanctions that the U.N has passed, because what is at risk is our national security. And there is only one way to shut a program down with a country like North Korea that doesn't have its own revenues. And I thank the gentleman from California for raising the point. And I yield back to him.

Mr. SHERMAN. I will just say that, for 20 years, we have talked about company sanctions instead of country sanctions. For 20 years, China has carried out a policy where they smile at us but they have done enough with North Korea so that their GDP is 50 percent higher in real terms. That is much better economic growth than we have achieved. So the sanctions have not prevented a high level of economic growth. And my guess is that we will continue the policies that we have in the past, perhaps at a louder volume.

And I would finally point out that we have to also remember how small the North Korean economy is, how difficult it is to squeeze. Yes, we are trying to go after their oil, but they use about the same amount of oil as 150 gas stations, total, the whole country. That is less than there are on Ventura Boulevard. And, of course, they can liquify their coal and use that in lieu of oil. So it is going to be tough to put this regime under enough pressure to even get a freeze. And the idea that we would ever get this regime—and having seen Saddam, having seen Qadhafi—to actually give up its nuclear weapons.

I yield back.

Chairman ROYCE. We go to Mr. Dana Rohrabacher of California, chairman of the Europe, Eurasia, and Emerging Threats Subcommittee.

Mr. ROHRABACHER. Thank you very much, Mr. Chairman. And thank you and Congressman Engel for providing the leadership on this committee to be dealing with issues of this magnitude. Thank you very much for your responsible leadership.

I share my colleague Mr. Sherman's frustration and skepticism that was just expressed. Let me note, my father was a Korean war veteran. And I would hope the very last thing that is on anybody's mind is to try to exercise more influence by putting more American troops in South Korea. That is not the path to a solution to this problem. So what are the solutions? I mean, obviously, we are being told, even from everything you are saying—in terms of economic sanctions, I agree with Mr. Sherman. I am very skeptical that any of that is going to have impact.

I remember being here and sitting a little bit over there at the time when President Clinton proposed and passed through this Congress a plan that would give the North Koreans billions of dollars of American assistance. Of course, we just did that with Iranians now too, with the same idea, that we are going to take some bloodthirsty tyrants and we are going to pay them off by giving them some sort of aid program for their countries.

So what is the solution? First of all, what is the challenge? Am I mistaken that I have heard quotes from the official head of the North Korean Government threatening to rain mass destruction of some kind upon the United States? Has he actually made threats to in some way kill millions of Americans with a nuclear attack?

Ms. THORNTON. I don't know if he said those specific words, but there certainly have been a litany of threats, including at Guam, including videos showing, you know, bombs raining on American cities. So I think——

Mr. ROHRABACHER. Okay. So he has made it clear that he is willing, as the leader of that country, to murder millions of Americans with the technology. Let me note, then, that I would hope, while we do not consider putting U.S. troops in South Korea as a solution, I would hope that we would be willing to use force, which is something that nobody seems to want to mention. And I think this is perhaps the only thing people like that understand.

And so I would suggest—I won't ask what type of force has been ruled out. And I am sure the administration has got the parameters of what type of force they are willing to use. But I would certainly think that the use of defensive forces—and, again, thank you, Ronald Reagan, for insisting that we have antimissile systems available.

I would hope that the next time the North Koreans launch a rocket, especially one that will traverse over our ally Japan, I would hope that we shoot it down as a message to the North Koreans and to other people, like in Japan, who are counting on us. And unless we demonstrate we are willing to use force, there is no reason for them to believe we will.

Also, not only an antimissile-defense type of approach, but I would hope that, if indeed another missile is launched, or they are preparing for a launch, that we conduct a cyber attack on North Korea. And, yes, it is a very small economy and a small country. A cyber attack against that type of threat should be effective, but it is a use of force without major loss of life, which is what Ronald Reagan talked about all the time. We don't want to be put in a position where our alternative is murdering millions of people who are basically the victims themselves of a totalitarian regime.

So I won't ask what parameters we have in the use of force, but let me just note, I don't believe that sanctions alone will have an impact on tyrants that murder their own family and have been so abusive and murderous to their own people. And I don't believe buying them off, as President Clinton tried to do—now we are stuck with this—down the road from that deal, we now have this. And those billion of dollars of assistance we gave North Korea, I would imagine, provided them other money that they could put into developing their own nuclear weapon system.

So, with that said, good luck to you all. Thank you very much. And thank you to our leadership in this committee. We are all Americans in this. Let's hope for the best but prepare for the worst.

Chairman ROYCE. Thank you, Mr. Rohrabacher. We now go to Mr. Gerry Connolly of Virginia.

Mr. CONNOLLY. Thank you, Mr. Chairman. And welcome.

We talk a lot about bipartisanship, and we want bipartisan on this committee and in our foreign policy. But we don't get bipartisan when we ignore history or when we whitewash the statements and actions of the current President with respect to North Korea.

We have a model that works—of course, a lot of people on this committee didn't support it—and that is called JCPOA, the Iran nuclear agreement. They have met the metrics. Recently, the United Nations certified they are complying. It rolled back a nuclear program. It involved cooperation not just with our allies but with our adversaries, Russia and China. And it had Iran at the table.

To what end is U.S. policy? What I didn't hear from my friends on the other side of the aisle, including the chairman in his opening statement, a powerful opening statement—I support tougher sanctions, always have. But it is one part of a policy, not the whole policy. As the Iran experience demonstrated, there has to be some reward for compliance and cooperation at the end of the day, or you are left with a policy only of talking loudly and carrying a stick.

We haven't talked about the fact—the ranking member did—that the President of the United States, in the midst of this crisis, threatened our ally, the most vulnerable party to North Korea's actions, South Korea, with abrogation of a free trade agreement we worked so hard to get. He accused the new South Korean President of appeasement. He threatened to cut off trade with any country that trades with North Korea. Well, that list is 80, including allies like India and Germany, Portugal, France, Thailand, the Philippines. Are we, in fact, going to cut off economic relations or trade with 80 nations? It is an empty threat. He talked about a response by the United States of fire and fury, but, frankly, the policy looks more like fecklessness and failure.

Ms. Thornton, is it the policy of the United States Government to abrogate the free trade agreement with South Korea? And has anyone at the State Department looked at the negative consequences of such an action, especially at this time?

Ms. THORNTON. Thank you, Mr. Connolly. Yes, we have looked very carefully at the Korea free trade agreement, KORUS. We are currently undergoing a very rigorous review of all the provisions. The United States Trade Representative recently held a——

Mr. CONNOLLY. My question—I am sorry. I am limited in time. Forgive me. My question is direct: Is it the position of the State Department that abrogating the free trade agreement with South Korea would be helpful in our diplomatic efforts and in our efforts to respond to the North Korean threat at this time?

Ms. THORNTON. No. I think what we would like to do is work to improve the trade agreement at the same time that we work with the South Koreans, obviously, on facing the North Korean——

Mr. CONNOLLY. Is it the policy of the State Department that the new President, President Moon, of South Korea is engaged in a policy of appeasement in any respect with respect to the north?

Ms. THORNTON. No. I think we have been working very hard to get the South Koreans to come around and be on the same page as we and the rest of our allies. And they have come around very nicely, I think.

Mr. CONNOLLY. Thank you. Mr. Billingslea, like you, I also served on the Senate Foreign Relations Committee and worked with your former boss, Mr. Helms. I was on the other side of the aisle. But we actually made a lot of music together sometimes, which always surprised the Reagan administration and the Bush administration afterwards.

You talked a lot about China. So China has been violating—and you provided some graphic evidence of that—with impunity, violating sanctions other flags shipping coal and providing badly needed foreign exchange for the North Korea regime. They just signed on in this unanimous U.N. resolution a new round of sanctions. Do we have any reason to believe that that would signal a change in Chinese behavior for the better, or is it another empty promise that will be violated with impunity?

Mr. BILLINGSLEA. To be determined.

Mr. CONNOLLY. Can you speak louder into your microphone?

Mr. BILLINGSLEA. Sorry, Congressman. It is to be determined. The reason I wanted to highlight for you the evasion schemes is that maritime enforcement now becomes crucial. With the two U.N. Security Council resolutions that are in effect, not sanctions but embargoes, complete embargoes, at least on paper, of coal, iron, lead, now textiles, seafood, gasoline, maritime enforcement of those U.N. Security Council resolution decisions, which are binding on all members of the U.N., that is going to be crucial going forward.

Mr. CONNOLLY. And if the chair would just indulge me for one followup question. So, at the end of the day—and either or both of you can answer. So let's say, by tightening sanctions, which I favor, we get North Korea to the table saying "Uncle," what do we give them in return? What are we prepared to do to entice North Korea, that there is, you know, a pot of something at the end of the rainbow if you freeze the program and start to reverse it under international observation?

Ms. THORNTON. I think——

Mr. CONNOLLY. Because isn't that the goal?

Ms. THORNTON. I will just be quick. I think the Secretary of State has been pretty clear in public remarks that we would be willing to look at economic enticements, at development opportunities for their economy, at their security concerns, and other things that we have talked about during negotiations with them in the past. And so I think all of that would be on the table, assuming we could get to—you know, we don't want to pay for negotiations or negotiate to get to the negotiating table. That is where we are right now.

Mr. CONNOLLY. At the end of the day, I will give you one word that has to guide U.S. foreign policy in all respects but especially North Korea. That word is "efficacy," which is defined as the ability to produce a desired and intended result. And I think that is also to be determined, Mr. Billingslea.

Thank you, Mr. Chairman, for your indulgence.

Chairman ROYCE. Thank you very much, Mr. Connolly.

We now go to Mr. Steve Chabot of Ohio.

Mr. CHABOT. Thank you, Mr. Chairman. And I want to again thank you and the ranking member, as others have said, for your at least attempts to get sanctions worked up. I think it is something worthwhile to pursue.

That being said, just one thing I wanted to make sure that I am accurate on this. Ninety percent, perhaps more, of what North Korea, the regime especially, needs to survive they get in one source or another from China. Is that—I am seeing nodding. Ms. Thornton, would you agree with that also? Okay.

That being said, obviously, China is the key, has been a long time, continues to be. It seems to me there are two things which could get China's attention. They have given us lip service for decades now, but one of those things is the trade with the U.S. is significant, and it seems that if we literally—I mean, some sanctions on banks, that may help a little bit, but it is not going to have the result, I think, that we all want, and that is to avoid military action and get North Korea to back off this march to madness in their nuclear program.

So one way is if we actually did cut off trade. And, of course, if we did that, would it have an adverse impact on the American economy? Of course it would. However, I would say that pales in comparison to the impact on the American economy if we see a thermonuclear device go off in Seattle or San Francisco or L.A. Or New York or Washington. So that is one thing that I think could actually get China's attention.

I think the other thing—and, Ms. Thornton, you sort of may have been at least thinking about this when you said that we are discussing with Japan and South Korea what they may want to move ahead on. And I don't know if this is what you had in mind or not, but it is certainly what I have in mind and have said this for years: They do not want Japan or South Korea to have their own nuclear programs. And I have thought for a long time that we should at least be discussing that with them. And I think the discussions alone could have gotten their attention, to get them to put pressure on North Korea to back off. It may be too late for that now. But could you comment on those two items which perhaps could get China to actually put sufficient pressure on North Korea to back away from this madness?

Ms. THORNTON. Sure. Well, I mean, we are certainly looking at every option to put more pressure on China. We are also using all of our global partners to speak up and also, from their perspectives, put pressure on China, because we do see China as the key to the solution of this problem, if we can get there.

As for cutting off trade, obviously that would be a huge step, and there are a lot of ramifications of that. I think going after entities and banks is a way of going more directly after the North Korean angle here, but I agree with you that, trade is preferable to seeing any kind of military confrontation, especially one that would involve people in the United States.

But on the issue of defenses in Japan and South Korea, we have certainly been talking to Japan and South Korea about beefing up their defenses and their ability to, themselves, take action in the event of an attack. And even those discussions have gotten China's attention. You probably know the Chinese have been very vocal about their opposition to the THAAD deployment in South Korea, which we have moved ahead on now and gone ahead and deployed over and above their objections. And we have made clear that the Japanese are seeking additional defensive systems to enable them to ward off a direct attack from North Korea. And it is quite clear, I think, already to the Chinese that this is an area that is going to be further developed if we can't rein in the threat from North Korea.

Mr. CHABOT. It is my view that, short of one of those two actions, I think we are going to continue down this path where Kim Jong-un will continue to move forward on this nuclear program. And that will leave only the military option, and there is no good to come from that. We know if we take that action, they can target Seoul, and literally tens, maybe hundreds of thousands of lives could be lost, including American lives. So that is the last resort, although it may ultimately come to that.

Or the alternative—some people are suggesting now, as well, we have a nuclear China, we have a nuclear Russia, we don't like that, so maybe we end up with a nuclear North Korea. Either one of you, why can we not allow that to happen? How are they different?

Ms. THORNTON. A lot of times, people talk about the North Koreans needing a nuclear program for their own defense. The fact of the matter is that there has been basically a mutual deterrence in effect since the end of the Korean War. They have a conventional position that allows them to target Seoul. And so the idea that they need nuclear weapons for their own defense, when there has never been a retaliation for any of their provocative, hostile, or even kinetic actions that they have taken, is a bit of a bridge too far.

So the concern is that they are pursuing a nuclear program in order to use that program to conduct blackmail and hold other countries hostage and continue to take even worse sorts of steps in their behavior. Proliferation is another major concern, of course. It undermines the entire global nonproliferation system and would be, we presume, ripe for sale and proliferation around the world. So I think two major angles there.

Mr. CHABOT. Thank you. My time has expired.

Chairman ROYCE. Mr. David Cicilline of Rhode Island.

Mr. CICILLINE. Thank you, Mr. Chairman. Thank you to our witnesses for being here.

I start with you, Ms. Thornton. You said, "We will never accept North Korea as a nuclear state." What did you mean by that? I mean, aren't they already a nuclear state?

Ms. THORNTON. No, we do not recognize them as a nuclear state. And——

Mr. CICILLINE. What does that mean?

Ms. THORNTON. We do not recognize them as a nuclear weapons state. We don't recognize their program, and we won't consider them to have nuclear weapons. We are pursuing denuclearization.

Mr. CICILLINE. Well, we can't imagine it away. Either they are a nuclear state or they are not. The recognition of one—I am not understanding that point. I mean, we have to have a realistic context before we can shape smart——

Chairman ROYCE. Will the gentleman yield for just a second?

Mr. CICILLINE. Sure.

Chairman ROYCE. Because there is an additional complexity here.

Mr. CICILLINE. About delivery.

Chairman ROYCE. Exactly.

Mr. CICILLINE. Yeah.

Chairman ROYCE. And I just wanted to make that point.

Mr. CICILLINE. No, no, I understand, but—okay. Let me move on.

Mr. Secretary, you said that U.N. Resolution 2371 prevents 55 percent of refined petroleum products from coming into North Korea and that new sanctions prevent $½ billion of coal, which leaves another $½ billion of coal and about 45 percent of petroleum products. Am I understanding that our sanctions don't reach the balance of that? And if not, why not?

Mr. BILLINGSLEA. So, Congressman, a couple of things. So all coal is prohibited to be transacted. That was under the prior——

Chairman ROYCE. Mr. Assistant Secretary, just pull the microphone a little closer.

Mr. BILLINGSLEA. Sorry. So, Congressman, it is not allowed to trade in North Korean coal, period, nor in iron, iron ore, lead, lead ore. North Korean——

Mr. CICILLINE. So those percentages relate to noncompliance.

Mr. BILLINGSLEA. The 55-percent number I gave you is kind of the fuzzy math done on how much gasoline versus crude oil is imported today into North Korea from China.

Mr. CICILLINE. Okay. Thank you. I think we have heard from a number of my colleagues in response to those questions about pretty clear noncompliance by the Chinese. The U.N. experts on North Korea in February found that they were using this livelihood exception to trade banned goods and allow companies to send rocket components to North Korea.

And you said, Ms. Thornton, and I think also Mr. Secretary, that we need to see that happen—that is, compliance by the Chinese. You described the Chinese as the center of gravity. And then, Ms. Thornton, you said, if China doesn't comply with the sanctions, we will use the tools at our disposal. What are those tools, and why aren't we already using them?

I mean, otherwise, these sanctions sound good in a press release, but if they are not actually being honored by the parties, they are not effective, as Mr. Connolly said. So what are the tools that you intend to use, and why aren't we already using them?

Ms. THORNTON. Well, one of the things to remember—I think the Assistant Secretary mentioned this—is that North Korea has been under sanctions for many decades. So their networks—it is a criminal enterprise, and their networks are deeply embedded, and they have designed them to escape detection. So it is a little bit complicated to go after these things.

But what I meant when I say using our tools, we have these international sanctions regimes. The international community has signed up to it and is obliged to enforce that. We have a running discussion with many of the countries around the world on information we have about what we find as illicit networks and ask them to go after those. If they don't, then we will use our domestic authorities to sanction those entities.

Mr. CICILLINE. I guess my question is, I think most military experts would acknowledge that there is not a good military option. We can talk about it, but there actually isn't one. And so, if we surrender the use of the sanctions regime to produce the result that we want, by not using every tool that is available to us, aren't we in the end acquiescing to North Korea's nuclear capabilities?

Ms. THORNTON. I think our strategy is to ramp up the sanctions regime, and that is exactly what we have been doing. We have had two unanimous U.N. Security Council resolutions in 2 months. That is unprecedented.

Mr. CICILLINE. No, no, I understand. But they have to be implemented in a meaningful way and fully. Otherwise, they are nice resolutions, but it sends the wrong message——

Ms. THORNTON. But that is exactly——

Mr. CICILLINE [continuing]. It seems to me, to North Korea if they don't see that that is real engagement by the Chinese to make these sanctions work.

Ms. THORNTON. Right. But that is exactly what we are working on. And I think, on sanctions regimes, a lot of people say the sanctions won't work either. But in past cases where we have used sanctions, I just want to note, you are a chump if you are implementing sanctions and they are not working until you are a genius when they do.

Mr. CICILLINE. No, no. I think sanctions do work if they are implemented. My last question is this. It seems to me that this suggestion that China is the center of gravity is right and that the only way that we will get China to fully implement the sanctions regime is for them to conclude that it is in their own interest to do that. And that will only happen when they arrive at the point that their fear of a unified Korean Peninsula aligned with the United States is outweighed by their fear of a military conflict on the Korean Peninsula. And I think that is the calculation.

And I guess my question is, what are the strategies that the administration is pursuing that bring China to that point where they conclude that it is in their interest to enforce the sanctions because the danger of a conflict on the peninsula is greater than their fear of some alignment by a unified Korean Peninsula with the United States? Or do you agree or disagree with that assessment? And I would ask Mr. Secretary and Ms. Thornton.

Ms. THORNTON. I think that that is right. And I think we have seen the Chinese moving in their system, for them, pretty swiftly toward a recalculation of what they are worried about on the Korean Peninsula. They see North Korea's actions undermining their own security through the beefing up of defenses in their region. They are certainly very alarmed at North Korea's behavior. And the explosion of the sixth nuclear test, the hydrogen bomb, right on their border is very concerning to them.

So I think we see them moving in this direction. It is not fast enough or sort of deep enough for us to be satisfied, but we are certainly pushing them in that direction. And we have an ongoing conversation with them about this at the highest levels.

Mr. BILLINGSLEA. I would also add that, as the chairman has pointed out, the Banco Delta Asia sanctions had a crippling effect on the regime, but that was more than a decade ago. We have for the first time in more than a decade taken action against, in this case, a Chinese bank. This was Bank of Dandong.

That was a very clear warning shot that the Chinese understood. And we are in repeated discussions with them that we cannot accept continued access in the international financial systems by North Koreans through their financial networks.

Mr. CICILLINE. Thank you. And I thank you, Mr. Chairman. I yield back.

Chairman ROYCE. Mr. Ted Yoho is chairman of our Asia-Pacific subcommittee. And he joined us in South Korea and has passed legislation to improve our ability to get information actually into North Korea. Mr. Yoho.

Mr. YOHO. Thank you, Mr. Chairman. And I thank you for holding this hearing today.

North Korea's recent provocations are its most dangerous yet. In launching a ballistic missile over Japan and detonating its most powerful nuclear device to date, the Kim regime has shown it is more emboldened than ever before. Kim Jong-un says we are backed into a corner. However, I think he is wrong. He is getting into a decreasing corner by his actions, and we are on the outside of that corner looking in.

But year after year, successive administrations have failed to fully implement the sanctions and China continues underwriting DPRK's programs, either financially via trade, doing 90 percent of their trade, or through technological exchanges, as we have seen with the rocket North Korea launched up and we recovered—or not we, but the South Koreans recovered the second stage and it was full of Chinese components. So China is complicit in this.

The implementation of the secondary sanctions authorized by Congress, as established, that we have done over the past years is often controversial, but as North Korea's nuclear technology has advanced, the need has become imminent. With these recent tests, implementation has been an existential need for millions of North Koreans, Japanese civilians, perhaps the United States, and really the world community.

And I find myself agreeing with my colleague Mr. Sherman again when he was talking about China. We have been here multiple times, his experience of 20 years in this committee, hearing the same story over and over again. And my questions are going to be focused on what do we do from this point forward.

You two are both in the seat that you are watching this at a very close level of engagement. You know what is working, what is not working. How do we go forward so that we are not back here in a year discussing what we should have done? I want to know what we did do and what tools you need to move forward so that these sanctions really do work.

Ranking Member Sherman and I both—we wrote a letter both to State and to the Treasury providing a list of Chinese banks that may have provided North Korean banks with indirect correspondence. And I am happy to say that the State Department have sanctioned recently—and China has been complicit with this and gone along with this—the Agricultural Bank of China and the China Construction Bank. These are great, positive moves, but there are still 10 more banks that China can sanction or put pressure on to stop doing business with North Korea.

And my question to you: Do you guys have enough tools in your arsenal to make sure that the world community—because it can't be just us. And that is why sanctions haven't worked in the past. It has to be a buy-in from the world community, because this is something that is affecting all of the world community, to get to a point where we have diplomacy that works so that we don't have any kinetic conflicts. Certainly, this world does not want to see a nuclear device go off in a homeland of anybody's. And this is this generation's fight, to make sure this doesn't happen. So, Ms. Thornton, is there anything else that you need that would make these other countries complicit with the sanctions?

Ms. THORNTON. Thank you very much, Mr. Subcommittee Chairman. We definitely believe that the U.N. Security Council actions are the most significant actions that we can take on the sanctions front, and that is because every country in the world is obligated to enforce those sanctions. It gives them the legal authority to do so, and it obliges them do so. And it opens up a whole sphere of enforcement for us to work with other countries on.

So I think the most significant actions in the U.N., which U.N. Security Council—our representative, Ambassador Haley, has undertaken, have been really key. The other key, I think, authorities are our domestic enforcement authorities, which back up the U.N. Security Council——

Mr. YOHO. Let me stop you there and ask you this. North Korea was on the state sponsors of terrorism list. And, certainly, we can look at their acts that they have done. In fact, you have said that North Korea was using intimidations, acts of intimidation—words you used to describe terrorism. So when we took them off the state sponsors of terrorism list, do you feel it would be important to put them back on that? And would it help toughen the sanctions and get compliance by the other countries?

Ms. THORNTON. I think the state sponsors of terrorism list is another statutory tool that we have, and, certainly, the Secretary is looking at that in the context of North Korea. I don't know that there are any——

Mr. YOHO. I am about out of time. Would it be prudent for us to——

Ms. THORNTON. I don't know if there are additional authorities there that would give us additional tools to go after things. I think it would be just another layer. But we are certainly——

Mr. YOHO. Another layer would be good.

Ms. THORNTON. Yes.

Mr. YOHO. And I appreciate your time. And I am sorry I didn't get to you, Assistant Secretary. I yield back. Thank you, Mr. Chairman.

Chairman ROYCE. Thank you, Mr. Yoho. We go now to Mr. Brad Schneider from Illinois, who was also with our delegation for our meetings with President Moon and other senior U.S. and South Korean officials during that time when the North Korean missile was shot over Japan.

Mr. SCHNEIDER. Thank you, Mr. Chairman. And, again, thank you for leading that delegation. It was an extraordinary opportunity to understand the situation better, to understand the threat, but also understand the strategy.

Today, we have talked a lot about strategy. We have talked about North Korea's strategy of accelerating testing, trying to miniaturize a weapon and put it on a missile. We have talked a lot about U.S. strategy and working within our laws as well as the United Nations.

But strategies follow goals. And we have had some discussion of our goals. If I could summarize our goals, it seems to be where priority number one is to eliminate the nuclear threat by North Korea. A secondary goal is to bring stability to the peninsula.

Ms. Thornton, you talked about what our goals are not. I just want to emphasize those. Not regime change or collapse; nor do we seek an accelerated unification of Korea or an excuse to send troops north of the armistice agreement's Military Demarcation Line. We have no desire to inflict harm on the long-suffering North Korean people, who we view as distinct from the hostile regime in Pyongyang. I think that is important. What I would like to ask you is if you could succinctly describe, what are North Korea's goals?

Ms. THORNTON. I think it is pretty hard to get inside the mind of the North Korean leader, but I think he has been fairly clear in public statements that he seeks to complete his nuclear weapons program in order to be able to sit down at the table with us as a sort of nuclear weapons fully developed state and——

Mr. SCHNEIDER. Well, that seems part of the strategy, but their long-term goals—Mr. Deputy Secretary?

Mr. BILLINGSLEA. I really do have to defer to State Department on this. My job is to drag them to the table through economic pressure. But I defer to State Department on any——

Mr. SCHNEIDER. Okay.

Ms. THORNTON. I think that most experts on Korea would say that the main, overarching goal—and I think one of the members mentioned the Juche philosophy, Representative Smith. I think that regime survival, regime perpetuation is pretty much an overarching purpose and goal.

Mr. SCHNEIDER. Okay. I mean, that seems to be the shared, collective wisdom. How about China? Because they have different goals, obviously, than ours, in many ways. How would you describe their goals in this dynamic?

Ms. THORNTON. I think China has been also pretty clear in their public comments that they don't want chaos, war, or nukes on the Korean Peninsula. Those are their stated three main goals in this particular issue. Of course, they are also looking to maintain stability in their region and to create the conditions for further economic development.

Mr. SCHNEIDER. Okay. So it seems that there is this shared perspective, at least between the U.S. and China, that achieving each of our respective goals—denuclearization, elimination of the nuclear threat—we should have—sanctions are the path to put pressure on Korea.

But how do we create—and this is a broad message, maybe, beyond here—a clear message for North Korea that the only path for survival, the only path for them to achieve their goals is through denuclearization, that they are taking the wrong path? What off-ramps, what mechanisms can we provide to show them that the way they are headed is a risk to their regime, a dire risk to their regime, every option being on the table, and that there is a different path and that path is open to them?

Ms. THORNTON. Well, it is difficult to do this when they are shooting ICBMs, threatening Guam, and exploding hydrogen bombs on the border of China. But I think we have been very clear in our public statements that denuclearization is the goal. We have used both words and actions to try to drive them in the direction that we want them to go—public statements by us, public statements by many of our partners and allies, in messages directly to the North Korean regime but also through public messaging, which the North Koreans definitely are picking up on, to tell them that denuclearization is the only path to survival for the regime.

And we have been quite explicit about that. We are trying to show them that through our deterrence actions, through our sanctions actions, through our diplomatic actions. And I think, you know, they have a different view so far, but we are continuing to press on that.

Mr. SCHNEIDER. And I don't mean this next question any other way than the way I am asking it. It really is an honest question. Is it better to have a very clear, consistent message that you take these steps, this is what we will do, or is it better, in your mind, to leave uncertainty and perhaps have a mix of messages?

Ms. THORNTON. Well, I think it is good to have consistent, clear messages, especially for a regime like North Korea that has a very opaque communication system and difficulty, probably, for information to reach the top leader, which is why we use public messaging in some cases, so that we can be sure that he can get it directly. But I think it is also important not to take any options off the table so that there is sufficient motivation for them to move toward the negotiating table.

Mr. SCHNEIDER. Yeah, I would share that. And I am out of time. I will ask a question maybe for later, someone else will touch on. We talked about the outside pressure in trying to get alignment with the U.S. and China in putting pressure on North Korea. But I would appreciate the opportunity for further discussion on how we create that internal pressure from within, not just making it harder for payment of the military, but for the public to understand what is really happening within North Korea and, in contrast, what the opportunities are without and pursuing that different path. And, with that, I thank you for the extra time, and I yield back.

Chairman ROYCE. Would the gentleman yield?

Mr. SCHNEIDER. Yes. Please.

Chairman ROYCE. I think you make a very important point, in terms of that focus. And there is another element, I thought, with respect to the conversations we have had. This is the second time we have talked to a senior North Korean defector who said, no, they already have the ability, they are not afraid of a South Korean attack or a North Korean attack because they have a million-man army on the border and the 100,000-plus missiles and all the other hardware.

What the issue is for North Korea is that they feel it is an illegitimate government in South Korea; that the founding of the Korean Peninsula, when the occupation was over from Japan, it should have been unified under the Kim dynasty. And the focus of the Kim regime, of Kim Jong-un, is on getting enough nuclear weapons, hydrogen bombs, that they can turn to Seoul and say, we are going to be reunified, but we are going to be doing it under the regime.

I think that is interesting information in that it comes from those who in one case was the head of propaganda for the regime. And if that is indeed the calculus, it really complicates things in terms of the feelings of the Kim regime. Both seemed to indicate that, although that was the focus of the Kim family, it may not necessarily be the focus of most North Koreans, who tend to understand that that drive to do that is what is costing the country its standard of living, its ability to give anyone else opportunity. It is solely in the interest of the megalomaniac who is currently in power.

I think that concept is an interesting one when it is shared with us by those who were actually part of the North Korean regime. But I do think we need to begin the process to having hearings to dig deeper into this whole calculus.

Mr. SCHNEIDER. And if I can, I think that is critically important. I couldn't agree more. And this is why I was talking about goals. If the goal is regime survival, that strategy, there is an opportunity to have—one direction. If the goal is the submission of South Korea, that is a different—the strategy can be the same with the development of nuclear weapons, but trying to create an opportunity for engagement is entirely different and much more challenging. So I think that is a critical conversation to have. Thank you.

Chairman ROYCE. Yes, indeed. Mr. Adam Kinzinger of Illinois.

Mr. KINZINGER. Thank you, Mr. Chairman. I just want to thank all of you for being here. And, personally, I want to commend the President, frankly, for finally taking a tough perspective on North Korea; I think, being very open about this is the challenge of our generation. We all know terrorism is a huge issue, but this is a bigger challenge. This is an existential threat, I would say, to the United States, to world order, to denuclearization of the world, to nuclear proliferation. And, as far as I see it, there are a lot of folks, and whether it is here at the hearing or if you watch the media, they all say there is no military option. They say, well, there is a military option, but not really; it is unthinkable, so we will never use it.

And I look at it this way: In order to actually achieve our objectives—and we have almost accepted defeat even prior to actually
going about these objectives, in some circles. We have three areas.
Number one is diplomacy, which we are ramping up in a big way
through economic use, through actual diplomacy, everything else.
Number two is missile defense, which we would obviously need in
the case that we have to defend ourselves. Number three is a military option. People that understand instruments of power and how
they work and the various instruments of power that our Nation
has to understand that you cannot do diplomacy with an adversary
without a big stick to use, whether that is military, whether that
is economic, whatever, that there has to be on the table basically
the unthinkable in order to make diplomacy work.

So, number one, diplomacy is good, but if we are ruling out a
credible military option, I think it is going to be unsuccessful ultimately. The idea of missile defense is great, and we need it. But
the reality is, if we just back up and say, well, as long as we build
a missile defense, North Korea will be allowed to have a nuclear
weapon, I think that leads to massive proliferation around the
world. How do you tell Iran that they can't have a nuclear weapon
when the JCPOA is up, actually fairly soon, when, in fact, you have
just given North Korea de facto access to a nuclear weapon?

And so let me just ask—I will ask a question, Mr. Billingslea, to
you. So when people go out and they say there really is no military
option, even though it is unthinkable—by the way, the military
should be used in doomsday scenarios, of which I think this ranks
up there with doomsday scenarios—does that strengthen your diplomatic hand, does that strengthen your ability to get North Korea
to the table, or does it weaken it?

Mr. BILLINGSLEA. I think we would be exceedingly unwise to take
anything off the table. I was a Senate staffer up here on the Foreign Relations Committee when the agreed framework was negotiated. And that was designed to freeze the Yongbyon reactor and
so on. And we gave all kinds of heavy fuel oil under the Clinton
administration. And look where we are now.

So this administration has made very clear, at the Cabinet level
and the President himself, that we are not going to kick this can
down the road. We can't. He is testing advanced nuclear designs
and ICBMs. It is a matter of time now before he mates the warhead to the missile and poses an existential threat not just to our
friends and allies but to us.

Mr. KINZINGER. Let me ask you a question to follow up. As a
prior administration official said—and I don't like to throw stones
at past administrations, so I am not doing that. But as this person
wrote in an op-ed, we have to just live with a nuclear North Korea,
in essence, for me, saying that the prior administration was willing
to live with a nuclear North Korea.

Let me ask you a question. If we say, as long as we have missile
defense, we are unwilling to do what is difficult for North Korea,
we are unwilling to engage in economic action against the Chinese,
push the Chinese back in their territorial disputes in the South
China Sea, whatever. If we do that, can you talk about what the
rest of the world will look like when we de facto accept North
Korea as a—even if we don't say we have accepted them, if we de

facto accept them, what does that do when the JCPOA runs out of time, what does that do to South Korea, Japan, other countries' nuclear ambitions, and what does that do to our moral authority to enforce the nuclear nonproliferation?

Mr. BILLINGSLEA. Well, I will defer to State Department on sort of the broader implications, but I would tell you, we are not willing to live with a nuclear North Korea. North Korea has proven that they are certainly willing to share nuclear technology with all manner of pariah regimes, to sell capabilities. I think Ambassador Bolton just had an op-ed where he pointed out it was a recent anniversary of the Israeli strike on a Syrian nuclear facility which was alleged to have been constructed with North Korean support, for instance. So these are big issues. We are determined to induce the Chinese to help solve this problem.

Mr. KINZINGER. Well, let me commend you on that. And, Ms. Thornton, I would give you the time; I am out. So I am not ignoring you. I just—the clock ran out. But let me say at the end, to reiterate what the Secretary said, I couldn't imagine in the situation that Syria is in today, which I think is tragic—and I think there has been a lack of action on our part to fix that—I couldn't imagine, had they had a nuclear program, what we would be looking at today.

And there is a lot of concern of social instability in North Korea. Look, people don't like to be oppressed. They won't be oppressed, even in a place like North Korea. What happens someday when that government is destabilized and you see something? I think these are all important questions.

And, again, I want to commend you and the administration and the State Department for their hard work on this issue. And I yield back.

Chairman ROYCE. We will go to Congresswoman Norma Torres of California.

Mrs. TORRES. Thank you once again, Mr. Chairman, for bringing us together for this very, very important and critical issue that we have here in dealing with North Korea and all of the problems that they have caused most recently.

I think we pretty much all agree that there is no magic bullet in dealing with this regime. And I think that we pretty much are in agreement that, so far, all the sanctions and everything that we have done hasn't worked. So where have we gone wrong? I don't know. Part of that we are trying to address here. I think that we have to be pretty realistic that this regime that we are dealing with is willing to do anything, put its people and the entire world at risk in order to achieve what they ultimately want to achieve, and that is a nuclear weapon that would come far enough to reach American citizens. And we have been talking a lot and calling out Los Angeles—I represent L.A. County—San Francisco. We haven't really mentioned Hawaii, which is a lot closer, and our territories.

Another issue that we have neglected to address, and that is the consumer issue. We haven't really engaged consumers and a more global inclusion to deal with North Korea and China's appetite to have slave-type workers working in their companies. So, as a consumer, when I am buying products, where is that chain of where this product was made and who it was made by? We know that many of our products are made in China, but not by whom. Correct?

So, to me, the bigger issue is, are we hitting the right targets? Are we being surgical enough to inflict the maximum pain on the regime versus inflicting the maximum pain on the people of North Korea?

Congresswoman Wagner and I have introduced the North Korea Follow the Money Act, H.R. 3261, which would direct the Director of National Intelligence to produce a national intelligence estimate of the revenue sources of the North Korean regime. My hope is that this bill will make our sanctions policy more precise and a bit more effective.

But I think that we still cannot get away from engaging, you know, more people. If foreign governments are not willing to engage—everyone is interested in a doomsday clock. It was advanced by another 30 seconds in January. And I think that we missed another opportunity to talk about what is happening in the Korean area more closely.

I would like to ask if you would agree that a clear picture of North Korea revenues—if we need to have a better picture of North Korea revenues in order for our sanction to be more effective.

Mr. BILLINGSLEA. So, Congresswoman, you are always going to find that I and the Treasury Department are interested in more intelligence, not less. We are an intelligence-driven organization, and the more precise information that can be generated, the better.

I would say that one—back to your point about opportunities missed. We are at the point now where enforcement is crucial. We have the various U.N. Security Council resolutions. In the past, it was sometimes very difficult to judge the proper enforcement of these different provisions because they weren't complete embargoes. You could get into arcane arguments about how much——

Mrs. TORRES. The best embargo that you can get is for the consumer to be more informed and for the consumer to say, I will no longer purchase any good that comes from this country——

Mr. BILLINGSLEA. One hundred percent.

Mrs. TORRES [continuing]. Because they are failing to support us in ensuring that we have a nuclear-safe world.

Mr. BILLINGSLEA. I agree 100 percent. And I would highlight two particular areas. You talked about labor. One of the successes that Ambassador Haley has had at the U.N. is getting past this idea that while we would just cap North Korean labor at whatever level it is, the slave labor in these various countries, we are now—under the new resolution passed last night, this is going to be wound down. That is important.

Seafood is the other area to really talk to consumers about to make sure that we go after any efforts to smuggle North Korean seafood into——

Mrs. TORRES. Can you give me an estimate of what percentage of North Korean revenues are from illicit sources?

Mr. BILLINGSLEA. At this stage, virtually all revenue is now illicit and illegal because the U.N. Security Council has banned just about every single——

Mrs. TORRES. So what are our options in dealing with that?

Mr. BILLINGSLEA. Maritime enforcement. The single most important thing we can do is enforce a complete prohibition on the sale of North Korean raw materials.

Mrs. TORRES. Thank you. My time has expired. I yield back.

Chairman ROYCE. We go now to Congressman Ted Poe of Texas.

Mr. POE. Thank you, Mr. Chairman. Thank you all for being here.

I think always when we make big decisions, we should look at history. My understanding is that the Russians, Stalin, put the Kim regime in power; first, to invade the South, in my opinion, to prevent the West being aware of what is taking place in Eastern Europe when the Soviet Union kept moving through and taking that area.

We have had three Kims in charge. They have all been very belligerent, they all have committed crimes, going all the way back to the hijacking of the Pueblo, to the KAL Flight 858, the attempted assassination of the South Korean President. They have a history of doing bad things. But it has always been the goal that they feel entitled because they are put there by Stalin to be in charge of North Korea. And as the chairman said, they want to concur the South. The war has never ended. It is a cease fire or a truce or an agreement not to—there is no treaty involved.

And we have been played by the Kims for years. They talk about causing war, nuclear capability, and the West says, oh, we will pay you not to do that if you promise to be nice. And so they promise not to declare war on anybody, they take our money, supposedly to feed their starving people, and then what do they do a few years later? They do the same thing. And this has been going on all the way back to the Clinton administration.

They understand one thing, that the West, the United States, can be bought off if they just make a lot of noise about doing bad things to the rest of us. We should understand that. We should understand that being nice and saying that we will take care of you and encouraging them in a diplomatic way to not declare war has not worked. And I'm not saying we ought to go to war, I am just saying that is what they understand.

So this President has taken a different point of view. He is talking in a language that I think little Kim can understand, that those days are over. And I commend Ambassador Nikki Haley for her work in getting these two latest rounds of sanctions through the U.N. The idea that the Chinese and the Russians are going to agree to sanctions on North Korea, I think that is a stroke of genius. I don't know how she did that. Especially the Russians, who started all of this with Stalin back in 1950.

So I want to know what our options are, not just one. I want to know where we are going. You know, we all want sanctions. Well, sanctions, they hadn't really done much to stop anything, but we want sanctions, and we want more sanctions, and we want little Kim to stop this. But what if he doesn't stop it? What is the U.S.'s plan? And surely the U.S. has a contingency plan down the road. What is it?

You all are looking at each other. What is the contingency plan? Sure, we want sanctions. We want to cripple the economy. We want them to stop the slave trade. We want them to do all those things.

But what have you done, because little Kim, he doesn't think like we do. So what are the rest of the options?

Ms. THORNTON. So, thank you. Yes, Mr. Congressman, I think we have a strategy. I mean, you all have heard from the Secretary, from other secretaries——

Mr. POE. What is it?

Ms. THORNTON. It is the pressure strategy. We want to solve this through negotiated settlement peacefully, but we are not taking any options off the table——

Mr. POE. Which are?

Ms. THORNTON [continuing]. Understand——

Mr. POE. I only have a minute, so you have to kind of cut to the chase. What are the other options?

Ms. THORNTON. Options to use force, options to use sanctions, pressure to choke off the regime's revenues, et cetera, to get them to come to the negotiating table. And I think we have been very clear about the strategy. We are not going to pay for negotiations, as has been done previously, as you mentioned. In past history, when we have dealt with the regime, they have sought payoffs. And we have made it very clear, the President and the Secretary, that we are not going to go down that road this time. We are going to band together with the coalition of global partners to choke off all of their economic revenue. And if we——

Mr. POE. So we have a military option down the road, if nothing works?

Ms. THORNTON. Sure.

Mr. POE. Would you agree with that, Assistant Secretary?

Ms. THORNTON. Yes. Absolutely. And as I said, we are not going to take any of those options off the table.

Mr. BILLINGSLEA. I would additionally offer, at a much more very precise level, and you will see it in my full written remarks, but we are targeting two things here. We are targeting his access to hard currency, because he needs these dollars for his WMD and missile programs. And we are targeting the way he still has access to the international financial system. We need to rip that out root and stem.

And that is what we are focused on, is shutting down his access to hard currency through these new U.N. embargoes that Ambassador Haley has successfully gotten in place. These are total cutoffs. You cannot trade in North Korean coal. That is a huge percentage of the revenue left to this dictator, given that we actually have relatively well shut off his arms trade and a number of the other things he was trading in. He has basically been reduced to high-volume, low-margin commodities, minerals, things like that, and we have to choke that off.

But, secondly, because of lack of enforcement in the international system by countries, we have talked about China today, Russia, he still has access to the international financial system because he has North Korean brokers and agents operating with impunity brazenly abroad in foreign jurisdictions. That has to stop. And so that is our next step.

Mr. POE. Thank you, Mr. Chairman, for the extra time.

Chairman ROYCE. Mr. Ted Lieu of California.

Mr. LIEU. Thank you, Mr. Chair. And, first of all, thank you to the witnesses for your public service.

I served on active duty under U.S. Pacific Command in the 1990s at Guam, and we did a whole series of different exercises, most of them were directed at North Korea, and it was really clear there were no good military options. And the reason I bring that up is because diplomatic economic options depends on whether, in fact, you have a good military option, and often it is not for us to say; it is dictated by the facts on the ground. And if we do have amazingly great military options, then we might do less diplomacy and less economic sanctions. But if we really have no good options militarily, then you might have to double down on what you are doing.

So I think it is important to just walk through some of those not so very good military options. And let me start with this question. The Trump administration's goal is to denuclearize North Korea. That is correct, right? But we don't know how many nuclear weapons they have. Isn't that correct?

Ms. THORNTON. We have estimates.

Mr. LIEU. Say that again.

Ms. THORNTON. We have estimates.

Mr. LIEU. You have estimates. And we also don't know where all those nuclear weapons are, correct? They are pretty good at hiding them.

Ms. THORNTON. They are good at hiding things.

Mr. LIEU. Right. So in order to get rid of those weapons to get the Trump administration's goal through military force, we would need a ground invasion, find those weapons, and destroy them. Isn't that correct?

Ms. THORNTON. Sorry, I didn't get the connection.

Mr. LIEU. Right. Since we don't know where the nuclear weapons are, we don't know how many they have. In order to denuclearize North Korea through a military option, we would need a ground invasion to find those weapons and destroy them. Isn't that correct?

Mr. BILLINGSLEA. I suspect we would need our Department of Defense colleagues here to really truly answer that.

Mr. LIEU. No, I understand. But for you to do your job, you also need to understand the military option, right?

So let me just go on. North Korea also has the knowledge to build nuclear weapons. Isn't that correct?

Ms. THORNTON. Yes.

Mr. LIEU. And they have got the knowledge to build ICBMs. And you can't unlearn that. So to keep them from doing this in the future, we would need to occupy the country or have South Korea or one of our allies occupy the country and keep them from doing this again in the future. Isn't that correct? If we were to do this through military force.

Mr. BILLINGSLEA. Well, I don't know that that is necessarily— and, again, I am putting my old Pentagon treaty negotiator hat on, but there are countries that have abandoned their nuclear programs and their missile ambitions. South Africa is a good example. Argentina is a good example. So there are examples.

Mr. LIEU. After the use of military force? No. Right?

Mr. BILLINGSLEA. Actually——

Mr. LIEU. Through other means. I mean, I can understand North Korea giving up or freezing the nuclear weapons, if we apply economic or diplomatic pressure. But what I am saying is if we were to use military force and they are going to resist it, and then to keep them from doing nuclear weapons in the future, we would need regime change to occupy the country. At least that is my sense. I don't know how we otherwise would do that. Let's just step away from nuclear weapons. They have also got about 5,000 tons of chemical weapons. Isn't that correct?

Ms. THORNTON. They do have chemical weapons, yes.

Mr. LIEU. Okay. And then they have this massive conventional arsenal of rockets and artillery and so on, correct? And they can launch all of that at South Korea. They can use missiles against Japan. They can use missiles against Guam, where we have got hundreds of thousands of Americans in those three areas, correct? And we have millions of civilians in all those areas, correct? So with any military option, we wouldn't be able to contain escalation. Isn't that correct?

Ms. THORNTON. It is all hypothetical, so I think it depends on things that are happening and it depends on a lot of other scenarios, but you are telling the story, so go ahead.

Mr. LIEU. Okay. So Defense Secretary Mattis has said, basically, there are no good military options, and the options would be very ugly, which then leads me to believe that your job is very critical. We essentially have diplomacy and economic sanctions. It seems like if we are going to proceed to diplomacy, might it not be a good idea to have an ambassador to South Korea that can help us?

Ms. THORNTON. Yes.

Mr. LIEU. Okay. Where are we with that? Why hasn't the President nominated an ambassador of South Korea?

Ms. THORNTON. We are working on it. I know the Secretary spoke to this the other day, I think. We are working on it.

Mr. LIEU. I am just saying it does send a message that we are not pursuing diplomacy seriously, and we are also disrespecting our critical ally, South Korea. And I urge the Trump administration to get its act together and nominate an ambassador to South Korea. With that, I yield back.

Chairman ROYCE. Thank you, Mr. Lieu. We go now to Mr. Lee Zeldin of New York.

Mr. ZELDIN. Well, Thank you, Mr. Chairman. And thank you to both of our witnesses for being here.

I believe that the administration has done a great job over the course of the first several months in office in making new strides, in bringing China to the table, to bring Russia to the table, to ramp up sanctions effort, to have more multilateral diplomacy, to have increased economic pressure, to engage in further information campaigns within North Korea that didn't exist previously. And I think Ambassador Haley, especially, deserves a whole lot of credit for her hard work at the United Nations with the success that she has achieved there. And we wish her nothing but the best.

Some of our colleagues have spoken about the idea of not using a military option. I think we all should agree that the military option should be the last possible option that we would be using after everything else were to fail. But some of my colleagues would go a little bit further, almost to suggest taking the military option off of the table. And I think from some of the other testimony here and your answers, there is certainly an agreement amongst others who would disagree believing that having the military option on the table is one that helps with multilateral diplomacy and increased economic pressure and all of the other efforts. So it would not be wise; it would be unwise to take the military option off of the table.

I wanted to ask you a little bit about what that red line is and has the administration taken a public position on a red line? Do you believe we should have one? What does it look like? Because, for me, the red line should be that North Korea should not have the ability to deliver a nuclear warhead to the United States. And there is still a component of their development that appears to not be there. The chairman got to it a little bit earlier as he was engaging one of our colleagues on the other side of the aisle as far as surviving reentry.

So we are pursuing the diplomacy angle. We are pursuing the economic angle and the information angle. Thinking of military option as the last possible option. Preparing the whole slate of conventional to unconventional military options. What is that red line?

Ms. THORNTON. Well, the assistant secretary and I are here representing the economic sanctions lever and the diplomatic levers in this. And I have said that we are determined to pursue a peaceful resolution through a negotiated settlement. Of course, we are not taking any options off the table. We realize this is a very difficult problem, as has been outlined by Congressman Lieu here.

I would say about red lines, we and the Secretary of State are determined to use this pressure campaign to get the North Korean regime to change its path and to come to the negotiating table with a serious set of proposals on denuclearization. How we verify that, complete verifiable, irreversible denuclearization is what we are seeking through a negotiated settlement.

I think we think we have a lot more room to go to squeeze them and increase the pressure of the international community. And I think we are continuing to see that that strategy is working, that the North Koreans are feeling that pressure. And we are focused on getting them back to the table.

So I think as far as red lines go for a military option, I would certainly want to defer that question to some future point where we are not as much engaged in the diplomatic and economic pressure part of the campaign.

Mr. ZELDIN. I personally believe that when the President said that North Korea would be met with fire and fury, that if North Korea were to attack the United States, they would be met with fire and fury. I was not offended, by any means. And I believe that Kim Jong-un needs to know. And as someone who is homicidal and not suicidal, he needs to know that he would be putting himself and his regime at great risk by attacking us.

There is a lot of hard work that has been done by the administration doubling down, tripling down, and quadrupling down, making a lot of progress, great progress specifically to the United Nations. I would just say if we truly want to prevent North Korea from having the ability to deliver a nuclear warhead to the United States, they are getting so much closer to it, that if we are actually serious about that military option, that we are going to have to start seriously having that discussion, because that may be imminent. I yield back.

Chairman ROYCE. Mr. Mike McCaul, who also chairs the Committee on Homeland Security.

Mr. MCCAUL. Thank you, Mr. Chairman. I appreciate that.

I view this as probably one of the biggest threats to the homeland, if they are capable of delivering an ICBM with a nuclear warhead to either Guam or the mainland of the United States. I know, looking back historically, A.Q. Khan and his network, this access between Pakistan, Iran, and North Korea. Once Pakistan got it, we couldn't take it away. Iran, we had our negotiations. And now, it looks like North Korea has it.

And I think once a country has this capability, it is very difficult to take it away. So I don't envy your positions in terms of trying to negotiate our way out of this. And I think the last previous administrations have failed to get us to that point, and now we are where we are. And I think Iran is probably watching this whole thing play out in terms of what is their next step going to be as well.

I am not going to get into military options. I know it is not your expertise. I do think cyber should be looked at as something that could be done to shut them down. And I know we have tremendous capability in that regard. But my question is—I know it has been talked a lot about Russia and China, are they going to cooperate with these sanctions, and how much leverage is China putting on North Korea. But my question really has to go to the more illicit side of the house.

Kim Jong-un has this North Korean Office 39 that raises—sells basically drugs, illegal exports of minerals, as you mentioned, counterfeit cigarettes, a lot of other things. What are we doing to try to counteract that? And, also, when it comes to proliferation and the sale of arms, can you tell me, how much do you estimate North Korea is making off proliferation to countries like Iran and Syria?

Mr. BILLINGSLEA. Congressman, it is good to see you.

Mr. MCCAUL. Yeah, you too.

Mr. BILLINGSLEA. So one of the things that is very important to underscore is that the Treasury Department and the authorities we wield are not, as you know from your time with the Department of Justice, they are not just sanctions. Sanctions is one of many tools we have. What we use to, in effect, collapse the Bank of Dandong was not a sanction; it was a—section 311 under the PATRIOT Act, action to root out the North Koreans in that bank.

In terms of the proliferation of weaponry, because of previous U.N. Security Council resolutions, we have been able to dry up much of the illicit sales that they were engaged in to various African regimes and so on. There are still several transactions that they periodically float that we are actively engaging various countries to deter signing of contracts and going down that road. It would be very unwise for them to take these actions. We are in a full court press on this.

Because of the success that Ambassador Haley and State Department have had at the U.N., in effect—you were asking about sort of illicit transactions—in effect, nearly every export coming out of

North Korea today, as of last night, nearly every export is now illicit. Textiles are now illicit. You cannot trade in North Korean textiles. You cannot trade in basic minerals anymore.

Under the previous administration, talking about bureau 39, one of the things they would do is sell these huge overpriced bronze statues, and then the weapons were the kicker on the side as a little sweetener for paying six times the going rate for a bronze statue. So that organization, the Mansudae Fine Arts Studio was sanctioned. And under our administration, we started rooting out the rest of that particular arts and monuments revenue-generating schema.

North Korean labor is another category that they are getting significant money from. And with the results last night, there is now not a freeze or a cap on North Korean laborers, there is a requirement to wind it down. I am not a big fan of wind-downs, because it is real hard to verify that. But that is, nevertheless, a big step forward, and we intend to enforce that as well.

I have reiterated on multiple occasions with counterparts in the Gulf and elsewhere that we need to see the North Koreans gone. The Department of State has been very active on this front, and we are seeing a drying up of revenue associated with the slave labor that the North Korean's employ.

Mr. McCAUL. And then to my last question, North Korea proliferating weapons to Iran and Syria.

Ms. THORNTON. So we do track any kind of illicit proliferation networks from the North Koreans and go after those transactions, again, with colleagues at Treasury and other agencies in the U.S. Government. When we find them, we try to block them or deter them. And we have had some success. It is a continuing effort on our part, and we devote a lot of attention to that in our Bureau of Nonproliferation.

Mr. McCAUL. But it is happening?

Ms. THORNTON. I think there are transactions that we are worried about, yes.

Mr. McCAUL. Okay. And I know some of that may be in another setting than this. So thank you very much.

Chairman ROYCE. Well, I want to thank the witnesses for their testimony. I thank you for answering the members' questions here today. I am sure more of those questions will be submitted for the record for you to answer. There are a few issues that are urgent for us, but I don't think any of them are more urgent than the North Korean threat at this time.

And to its credit, the administration recognized this early on. Secretary Tillerson's first focus as Secretary of State was North Korea. And he has been extensively engaged, working with allies in the region, while pressuring China and Russia and other countries that are funding the Kim regime. We need more sanctions, tougher sanctions. We need to supercharge this right now. And the administration is moving in the right direction. And China, each day, is rethinking the cost of its financial support for North Korea.

The administration's focus on Korean slave labor abroad is very good. Sanctions are just one element of power we need to bring to bear. We need to stop giving only lip service to the power of information inside North Korea, broadcasting information in to change attitudes and conditions in North Korea. We simply aren't doing this well enough, and it must be a priority.

And, again, thank you for your testimony. We look forward to your follow-up, and this hearing stands adjourned.

[Whereupon, at 12:25 p.m., the committee was adjourned.]

APPENDIX

Material Submitted for the Record

FULL COMMITTEE HEARING NOTICE
COMMITTEE ON FOREIGN AFFAIRS
U.S. HOUSE OF REPRESENTATIVES
WASHINGTON, DC 20515-6128

Edward R. Royce (R-CA), Chairman

September 12, 2017

TO: MEMBERS OF THE COMMITTEE ON FOREIGN AFFAIRS

You are respectfully requested to attend an OPEN hearing of the Committee on Foreign Affairs, to be held in Room 2172 of the Rayburn House Office Building (and available live on the Committee website at http://www.ForeignAffairs.house.gov):

DATE: Tuesday, September 12, 2017

TIME: 10:00 a.m.

SUBJECT: Sanctions, Diplomacy, and Information: Pressuring North Korea

WITNESSES: Ms. Susan A. Thornton
                    Acting Assistant Secretary
                    Bureau of East Asian and Pacific Affairs
                    U.S. Department of State

                    The Honorable Marshall Billingslea
                    Assistant Secretary
                    Office of Terrorism and Financial Intelligence
                    U.S. Department of the Treasury

By Direction of the Chairman

COMMITTEE ON FOREIGN AFFAIRS
MINUTES OF FULL COMMITTEE HEARING

Day__*Tuesday*__Date____*09/12/2017*____Room____*2172*____

Starting Time _*10:05AM*_ **Ending Time** _*12:30PM*_

Recesses | *0* | (____to ____) (____to ____) (____to ____) (____to ____) (____to ____) (____to ____)

Presiding Member(s)
Chairman Edward R. Royce

Check all of the following that apply:

Open Session ☑
Executive (closed) Session ☐
Televised ☑

Electronically Recorded (taped) ☑
Stenographic Record ☑

TITLE OF HEARING:

Sanctions, Diplomacy, and Information: Pressuring North Korea

COMMITTEE MEMBERS PRESENT:

See attached.

NON-COMMITTEE MEMBERS PRESENT:

N/A

HEARING WITNESSES: Same as meeting notice attached? Yes ☑ **No** ☐
(If "no", please list below and include title, agency, department, or organization.)

STATEMENTS FOR THE RECORD: *(List any statements submitted for the record.)*

Mr. Connolly

TIME SCHEDULED TO RECONVENE ________
or
TIME ADJOURNED *12:30PM*

Full Committee Hearing Coordinator

HOUSE COMMITTEE ON FOREIGN AFFAIRS
FULL COMMITTEE HEARING

PRESENT	MEMBER	PRESENT	MEMBER
X	Edward R. Royce, CA	X	Eliot L. Engel, NY
X	Christopher H. Smith, NJ	X	Brad Sherman, CA
	Ileana Ros-Lehtinen, FL		Gregory W. Meeks, NY
X	Dana Rohrabacher, CA		Albio Sires, NJ
X	Steve Chabot, OH	X	Gerald E. Connolly, VA
	Joe Wilson, SC		Theodore E. Deutch, FL
X	Michael T. McCaul, TX	X	Karen Bass, CA
	Ted Poe, TX		William Keating, MA
	Darrell Issa, CA	X	David Cicilline, RI
	Tom Marino, PA		Ami Bera, CA
	Jeff Duncan, SC		Lois Frankel, FL
X	Mo Brooks, AL	X	Tulsi Gabbard, HI
	Paul Cook, CA	X	Joaquin Castro, TX
	Scott Perry, PA		Robin Kelly, IL
	Ron DeSantis, FL		Brendan Boyle, PA
	Mark Meadows, NC		Dina Titus, NV
X	Ted Yoho, FL	X	Norma Torres, CA
X	Adam Kinzinger,IL	X	Brad Schneider, IL
X	Lee Zeldin, NY		Tom Suozzi, NY
	Dan Donovan, NY		Adriano Espaillat, NY
	James F. Sensenbrenner, Jr., WI	X	Ted Lieu, CA
	Ann Wagner, MO		
	Brian J. Mast, FL		
X	Brian K. Fitzpatrick, PA		
	Francis Rooney, FL		
	Thomas A. Garrett, Jr., VA		

Statement for the Record
Submitted by Mr. Connolly of Virginia

On September 3, the North Korean regime conducted its sixth and most powerful nuclear test to date, involving its first true thermonuclear device – "the hydrogen bomb." The Democratic People's Republic of Korea (DPRK) now claims that it has technical knowledge of a two-stage thermonuclear warhead, meaning that it can mount a miniature hydrogen bomb on an intercontinental ballistic missile (ICBM). The regime's drive to become a nuclear power presents a real and dangerous threat to U.S. national security and that of our allies. Our priority must be to de-escalate tensions on the Korean Peninsula by providing steady leadership, reassurance for our allies, and a comprehensive strategy with carrots and sticks to bring North Korea to the negotiating table. Instead, the Trump Administration is destabilizing an already volatile situation with bellicose rhetoric, uninformed and conflicting messages, and attacks on our allies.

With tensions flaring, President Trump warned that he would meet North Korean threats with "fire and fury like the world has never seen." But frankly, his response looks more like fecklessness and failure. Just as he has been with Iran, the President appears to be singularly focused on military solutions to this intractable global flashpoint on the Korean Peninsula. His administration has proposed dramatic increases to the defense budget offset by an evisceration of our diplomatic capabilities, and he has failed to make key diplomatic appointments, including an Ambassador to Seoul and an Assistant Secretary for East Asian and Pacific Affairs. The President's inflammatory rhetoric and failure to resource U.S. diplomatic efforts are more likely to blunder us into war than set the stage for peace.

Now, it is more important than ever to stand strong with our allies, especially South Korea and Japan, and project a unified front. Amidst this extreme volatility on the Korean Peninsula, Trump has declared his intent to withdraw from the U.S.-Korea Free Trade Agreement (KORUS), dealing a heavy blow to U.S.-Republic of Korea (ROK) relations, our 6th largest trading partner. The President also criticized South Korea for its "talk of appeasement with North Korea." I recently joined my fellow co-chairs of the Congressional Caucus on Korea to write to the president and rebuff him for opening fissures in the U.S.-ROK alliance – an alliance forged in blood – which has served U.S. security interests in the region and acted as a guarantor for the safety of 50 million South Koreans.

Following the most recent nuclear test, Trump suggested ending all trade with countries doing business with North Korea. Around 80 countries traded with Pyongyang in 2016, including China, Russia, India, Pakistan, Singapore, Germany, Portugal, France, Thailand and the Philippines. If the U.S. ended trade with China alone, we would forego 4.4 percent of U.S. GDP, compared to just 0.92 percent lost due to the Great Recession in 2008. Cutting off trade with 80 nations is an empty threat.

We need to discuss a credible and comprehensive strategy that includes defensive military measures, economic pressure, and diplomacy. Last week, South Korean President Moon Jae-in reversed his opposition to the Terminal High Altitude Area Defense (THAAD) system and completed the deployment of four additional launchers. THAAD provides a shield against ballistic missiles launched from north of the 38th Parallel.

In August 2017, the President enacted the Countering America's Adversaries Through Sanctions Act (P.L. 115-44), which is the strongest sanctions regime ever passed by Congress. This hard-fought measure updates and expands the North Korea Sanctions Policy Enhancement Act of 2016 (P.L. 114-122) that was enacted last year. It authorizes new sanctions provisions related to sanctions evasion, the use of North Korean exported labor, correspondent banking, and trade in oil, textiles, and food and agriculture products. The bill included my amendment, which will ensure that U.S. sanctions against North Korea do not impede the provision of vital U.S. assistance to developing countries for maternal and child health, and disease prevention and response.

U.S. sanctions are a necessary but insufficient tool to address the threat of North Korea's weapons program. The United States must undertake a rigorous diplomatic effort to urge the global community, and China in particular, to fully enforce international sanctions on North Korea. On September 11, the U.N. Security Council unanimously passed UNSCR 2375 against North Korea in response to its latest nuclear test. The resolution reduces Pyongyang's oil/petroleum imports by thirty percent, bans all textile exports, and prohibits new work permits for North Korean workers.

The Korean Peninsula remains one of the most dangerous flashpoints on the globe. Navigating this complex web of regional stakeholders and competing interests will require patient and committed U.S. leadership to avert the ever-present potential of conflict that looms over 75 million Koreans. We have accomplished such diplomatic feats before, most recently through the Joint Comprehensive Plan of Action (JCPOA), which reversed the Iranian nuclear program. I look forward to hearing from our witnesses today regarding how best to achieve our nonproliferation goals for the Korean Peninsula.

Questions for the Record Submitted to
Acting Assistant Secretary Thornton by
Representative Eliot Engel
House Foreign Affairs Committee
September 12, 2017

Question:

The Trump Administration says that North Korea is their top foreign policy priority. However, with vacancies across the interagency including the Department of State, what Senior Administration official in the U.S. government is taking the lead on driving North Korea policy? Does this person have sufficient rank and relationship to the White House to be perceived as credible to the North Koreans as speaking for the U.S. government?

Answer:

The President's top priority remains protecting the homeland, U.S. territories, and our allies against North Korean aggression. The Department of State is devoting substantial resources to ensure strong enforcement of our DPRK policies, including better implementation of sanctions already in place.

The Secretary considers DPRK amongst our most urgent priorities. He has been leading overall department efforts. Ambassador Joseph Y. Yun is our Special Representative for North Korea Policy and has coordinated Department efforts in support of the Secretary's strategy. Ambassador Yun brings significant experience and expertise on North Korea to the table, having worked on this issue in various roles throughout his career, most notably while previously serving as the Principal Deputy Assistant Secretary in the Bureau of East Asian and Pacific Affairs. Ambassador Yun, with the support of Secretary Tillerson and Deputy Secretary Sullivan, is actively leading our peaceful pressure campaign to apply maximum diplomatic and economic pressure on North Korea to convince its government to cease its unlawful, dangerous, and destabilizing actions, to reduce tensions in North East Asia, and to end its prohibited nuclear weapons and ballistic missile programs.

Question:

While Secretary of State Tillerson proposes elimination of the Special Envoy for North Korean Human Rights, the Secretary of Defense and National Security Advisor are urging greater diplomatic effort in our approach toward the North. Officials serving in this position over the last several years have succeeded in getting a U.N. Commission of Inquiry on North Korea that contributed to the United States designating Kim Jung Un personally for his egregious human rights violations. Does Secretary Tillerson see human rights as an important aspect of U.S. policy toward North Korea? If so, given the global duties of the Under Secretary for Civilian Security, Democracy and Human Rights is there time to focus meaningful attention on North Korea?

Answer:

I can assure you that this Administration remains deeply concerned by gross human rights violations and abuses committed by the North Korean government, which were clearly documented in the 2014 UN Commission of Inquiry's report. In July, Secretary Tillerson highlighted the regime's systematic use of forced labor to generate illicit revenue and our pressure campaign has sought to end the regime's exportation of labor through diplomatic pressure and the two most recent UNSCRs.

Our strategy to promote human rights in North Korea focuses on three core objectives, including increasing international awareness, expanding access to independent information, and promoting accountability for those responsible for human rights violations and abuses in North Korea. We support the free flow of independent information into, out of, and within the isolated nation so the North Korean people have access to voices of freedom and democracy, and greater visibility into current events inside their country and in the outside world.

The Secretary believes that integration will make knowledge and resources more accessible, provide clarity in reporting authority, strengthen communication channels, and create a more efficient and integrated diplomacy. By dual hatting the North Korea Human Rights Envoy position with the Under Secretary for Civilian Security, Democracy and Human Rights, we will realign the position within the family of bureaus focused on issues within the envoy's mandate. The title would remain and would continue to be a position confirmed by the Senate, consistent with the applicable statutory requirements.

Question:

Notwithstanding recent designations, we still have a long way to go before we are exerting "maximum pressure" on North Korea's economic interests. Open-source researchers have demonstrated that there is a <u>centralized, limited and vulnerable network</u> of third-party gateway firms in China and elsewhere that form North Korea's illicit network.

- Can the U.S. identify the top 20-30 firms that compose North Korea's illicit network? Please provide that information, in classified form if necessary.

- It is my understanding that most of these entities operate in China and a small number of other jurisdictions. Have we informed Beijing (and/or the relevant governments) of the activities of these entities and unequivocally communicated the expectation of the U.S. government that their actions be curbed?

- Please provide, in classified form if necessary, a detailed accounting of all the cases you have raised with China and Russia (and/or the relevant governments)?

- China and Russia (and/or the relevant governments) have not taken sufficient action to close these entities and curb their activities, what action has our government taken to designate these entities under U.S. law? If not, what is the impediment to doing so in each case?

Answer:

Regarding China, it is well known that over 90% of the DPRK's exports go through or to China. That is a lot of economic leverage. That is why we have told the Chinese that their willingness to cooperate with us to solve the Asia Pacific region's most acute threat to peace and stability will be a benchmark of its commitment to pursue constructive, results-oriented relations with the United States. If they so choose, this can be a highlight of bilateral cooperation.

China pledged to work with the United States on North Korea during the President's April meeting with President Xi Jinping. In total, China has endorsed seven UN Security Council resolutions on the DPRK since 2006, six of which included increasingly robust sanctions.

Following its earlier suspension of DPRK coal imports – depriving the regime of its largest coal export market and diminishing its single largest source of revenue – China announced a comprehensive ban on the import of coal, iron, iron ore, lead, lead ore, seafood, and aquatic products effective August 15 in compliance with UNSCR 2371.

In fact, we have seen reports that Chinese banks have adopted stronger measures to protect themselves from DPRK connections that would make them vulnerable to economic measures by the United States. While we defer to Treasury on the status of the rule proposed against the Bank of Dandong, the reputational cost of doing business with the DPRK has been made clear.

Of course, we would like to see China do more, even above and beyond the most recent UNSCRs' provisions. The UN Security Council has designated dozens of DPRK entities, many of which do business through China, and we're working with China to implement these UN Security Council resolutions. In particular, we are pushing for robust implementation of UN Security Council Resolution 2371 and 2375 by China, which would remove up to a billion dollars from North Korea's annual export revenue—money that North Korea might otherwise use to fund its WMD programs.

We remain clear-eyed about China's track record on North Korea and will continue to carefully monitor Chinese compliance with these agreements. We have told the Chinese in no uncertain terms that we will utilize all tools at our disposal, including U.S. sanctions, to choke off resources that fund the DPRK's proscribed nuclear, missile, and other WMD programs. The U.S. and China regularly exchange information on particular cases of concern in implementing UNSCRs. In some cases, China has taken its own action against illicit DPRK entities.

The following is a list of some examples highlighting actions that our government has taken to target North Korean entities working in China, Russia or other locations, as well as Chinese and/or Russian entities that provided financial or relevant assistance to North Korea:

- On September 26, the Department of the Treasury designated eight North Korean banks and 26 individuals and identified two banks as part of the Government of North Korea, in response to North Korea's ongoing development of weapons of mass destruction (WMD) and continued violations of United Nations Security Council resolutions (UNSCRs). Pursuant to Executive Order (E.O.) 13687 and E.O. 13810, issued on September 20, 2017, these actions target North Korean nationals operating in Libya, United Arab Emirates, China, and Russia who act as representatives of North Korean financial institutions.

- On August 22, the United States announced 16 new sanctions designations targeting third-country companies and individuals, including in China and Russia, which operate in North Korea's coal, energy, shipping, and labor sectors, all of which generate revenue for the regime's weapons of mass destruction programs.

- These designations follow the Department of the Treasury's finding announced June 29 that Bank of Dandong, a Chinese bank that acts as a conduit for illicit North Korean financial activity, is a foreign bank of primary money laundering concern. In addition, Treasury's Office of Foreign Assets Control (OFAC) designated two Chinese individuals and one Chinese company in response to North Korea's ongoing WMD development and continued violations of UN Security Council resolutions.

- Furthermore, on June 1, 2017, the Treasury Department designated a Moscow-based company and its director for their support for a procurement company involved with North Korea's WMD and missile programs. Treasury also designated Russia-based Independent Petroleum Company and one of its subsidiaries for involvement in the North Korean energy industry and possible sanctions evasion activities. As part of this tranche, the State Department also designated two North Korean proliferation-related entities.

- On September 26, 2016, the Department of Justice unsealed a criminal complaint against a Chinese company, Dandong Hongxiang Industrial Development Co., and four Chinese nationals for: conspiracy to violate the International Emergency Economic Powers Act (IEEPA) and defraud the United States; conspiracy to launder monetary instruments; and violation of IEEPA. The Department of Treasury designated these same entities under E.O. 13382 which targets weapons of mass destruction proliferators and their supporters.

Question:

We know China is violating the UN sanctions it agreed to in the United Nations Security Council. The United Nations Panel of Experts on North Korea found in February that China has used so-called "livelihood exemptions" to trade banned goods and allow its companies to send rocket components to North Korea. What is the administration's plan for holding Chinese entities accountable for Sino-North Korean business transactions that violate existing sanctions? What metrics will the administration use to determine when more secondary sanctions are necessary and how broad those measures should be?

Answer:

Over 90% of the DPRK's exports go through or to China. That gives China significant economic leverage. That is why we have told the Chinese that Beijing's willingness to cooperate with us to solve the Asia Pacific region's most acute threat to peace and stability will be a benchmark of its commitment to pursue constructive, results-oriented relations with the United States. If they so choose, this can be a highlight of bilateral cooperation.

We have told the Chinese clearly and repeatedly that we will use all tools at our disposal, including U.S. sanctions, to choke off resources that fund the DPRK's proscribed nuclear, missile and other WMD programs. We want to work with China, but we've said many times that we will not hesitate to act alone, including by sanctioning Chinese or other third-country individuals and entities that provide support to North Korea's unlawful activities. In short, this Administration will go wherever the evidence leads to impose legally available sanctions on entities or individuals that support North Korea's proscribed programs.

Question:

Some experts assert that Beijing is playing a "double game" whereby they agree to certain sanctions at the UN but then fail to enforce them. Meanwhile, as other countries do take actions to cut off ties with North Korea, China simply picks up the slack. China has a responsibility to be transparent and provide the international community with detailed, real-time information about their trade with North Korea. Crude oil appears to be North Korea's largest import from China, but China stopped reporting crude oil shipments in 2014. China is North Korea's gateway to the world -- what are we doing to hold China accountable for providing real-time data transparency on both sanctions enforcement as well as their "licit" trade with North Korea?

Answer:

We remain clear-eyed about China's track record on North Korea and will continue to carefully monitor Chinese compliance with UN Security Council Resolutions. We have told the Chinese clearly and repeatedly that we will use all tools at our disposal, including U.S. sanctions, to choke off resources that fund the DPRK's proscribed nuclear, missile, and other WMD programs. The United States and China regularly exchange information on particular cases of concern in implementing UNSCRs, and, in some cases, China has taken its own action against illicit DPRK entities. China has published customs and other trade data about its trade with North Korea in nearly all circumstances and in nearly all sectors, and we work bilaterally with China and through our own intelligence analysis to monitor China's implementation of the UNSCRs.

Question:

Two of China's poorest provinces, Liaoning and Jilin, border North Korea, and China has put forward trade with North Korea as a path to greater economic growth. Today, the development plan for the provinces lay out policies designed increase trade with North Korea. At a time when the international community is trying to cut off sources of hard currency to the Kim regime, is it reasonable to expect compliance from officials in Northeastern China? Given Beijing's concerns about stability, is it not more likely that the central government will look the other way and allow cross-border trade to continue?

<u>Answer:</u>

We remain clear-eyed about China's track record on North Korea and will continue to carefully monitor Chinese compliance with UN Security Council Resolutions. We have received recent reports about stepped-up enforcement by China's central and local government in its Northeastern provinces bordering North Korea, especially since the adoption of UNSCRs 2371 and 2375. For a country that has is a conduit for 90% of North Korea's exports, China is bound to bear a disproportionate burden – and responsibility – in implementing the UNSCRs. In this context, we are closely monitoring China's compliance with UN Security Council Resolutions.

Questions for the Record Submitted to
Mr. Marshall Billingslea
House Foreign Affairs Committee
"Sanctions, Diplomacy, and Information: Pressuring North Korea"
September 12, 2017

<u>**Representative Eliot Engel**</u>

1. Russia has recently emerged along with China as opposing further sanctions at the United Nations and some believe that Putin is giving Xi space to navigate. Additionally, there are reports Russia is providing materials to North Korea for their nuclear program. Do we have evidence of Russian components or technology and what the North Koreans are using to develop their weapons? What is that evidence and how have we acted on this knowledge?

   Answer:
   Russia is to be recognized for supporting the adoption of the most recent UN Security Council Resolution. Nevertheless, they can and must do more to implement and enforce UN sanctions. Treasury is committed to targeting any Russian individuals and entities providing support to North Korea.

   In June and August 2017, Treasury designated Russian individuals and companies involved in supporting the UN- and U.S.- designated Korea Tangun Trading Corporation (Tangun), also known as Korea Kuryonggang Trading Corporation. OFAC designated Moscow-based Gefest-M LCC and its director, Russian national Ruben Kirakosyan, as well as Moscow-based Ardis-Bearings LLC and its director, Igor Aleksandrovich Michurin. Tangun is responsible for the procurement of materials in support of North Korea's WMD and delivery systems programs and have been involved in procurements for Tangun's Moscow Office.

   In June and August 2017, Treasury designated Russian individuals and companies involved in selling petroleum to North Korea. In June, Treasury designated the Independent Petroleum Company, a Russian company that has reportedly shipped over $1 million worth of petroleum products to North Korea. In August, Treasury designated three Russians who were also involved in providing gasoil to North Korea.

   Treasury will continue to investigate and target individuals and entities that provide support to North Korea's economy.

2. Notwithstanding recent designations, we still have a long way to go before we are exerting "maximum pressure" on North Korea's economic interests. Open-source researchers have demonstrated that there is a centralized, limited and vulnerable network of third-party gateway firms in China and elsewhere that form North Korea's illicit network.

   a. Can the U.S. identify the top 20-30 firms that compose North Korea's illicit network? Please provide that information, in classified form if necessary.

Answer:

    Open source research, when it contains primary source material such as corporate registrations, ownership structure, and company literature, can be extremely useful in mapping illicit networks. The Treasury Department actively works to map out North Korea's financial and revenue-generating mechanisms. North Korea employs deceptive financial practices and is constantly adapting to U.S. sanctions. Therefore, the Treasury Department is constantly investigating North Korea's financial networks as they change. We do not hesitate to use open-source due diligence products as part of our effort. We would be happy to provide a classified briefing on this matter.

b.   It is my understanding that most of these entities operate in China and a small number of other jurisdictions. Have we informed Beijing (and/or the relevant governments) of the activities of these entities and unequivocally communicated the expectation of the U.S. government that their actions be curbed?

Answer:

    Treasury leadership regularly engages with Chinese government representatives to find ways in which we can work together to implement and enforce UN Security Council Resolutions, with a view toward restricting the North Korean regime from acquiring and accessing the revenues it needs to fund its nuclear program.

    This includes times when I and other Treasury leadership engage with Chinese government officials on specific entities that we believe are associated with North Korea. Nevertheless, the time for incremental changes has passed. We are now pushing the Chinese government to conduct a widespread crackdown on trade with North Korea, and to ensure that Chinese banks are not holding accounts for North Korean financial facilitators.

c.   Please provide, in classified form if necessary, a detailed accounting of all the cases you have raised with China and Russia (and/or the relevant governments)?

Answer:

    While we defer to the Department of State on furnishing details to its oversight committee, we stress that the Treasury Department is committed to rapidly increasing economic pressure on North Korea. Time is not on our side. We can no longer slowly prod countries to expel North Korean trade and financial representatives one at a time. We are at the point where widespread and swift action by China and Russia is needed to curtail any economic relationship with North Korea.

    On September 26, Treasury designated twenty-six North Korean financial facilitators. Nineteen of them were operating in China and three were based in Russia. Under UNSCR 2321, adopted in November 2016, UN Member States are required to expel North Korean banking officials, if a Member State determines that an individual is working on behalf of or at the direction of a North Korean bank or financial institution. These designations demonstrate our commitment to action.

d.   China and Russia (and/or the relevant governments) have not taken sufficient action to close these entities and curb their activities, what action has our government taken to designate these entities under U.S. law? If not, what is the impediment to doing so in each case?

Answer:

As described above, the Treasury Department is actively targeting North Koreans operating in China. We are also targeting Chinese and Russian individuals and entities providing economic support to North Korea. Treasury's sanctions are not intended to punish China and Russia; they are intended to stop individuals and entities from cooperating with North Korea and prevent North Korea from accessing the U.S. financial system. When we see instances of sanctions evasion, we will act.

3.   We know China is violating the UN sanctions it agreed to in the United Nations Security Council. The United Nations Panel of Experts on North Korea found in February that China has used so-called "livelihood exemptions" to trade banned goods and allow its companies to send rocket components to North Korea. What is the administration's plan for holding Chinese entities accountable for Sino-North Korean business transactions that violate existing sanctions? What metrics will the administration use to determine when more secondary sanctions are necessary and how broad those measures should be?

Answer:

On September 20, the President issued Executive Order (E.O.) 13810, greatly expanding Treasury's sanctions authorities and expressly authorizing Treasury to use secondary correspondent account sanctions in the North Korea program. For example, E.O. 13810 allows Treasury to suspend or restrict U.S. correspondent account access to any foreign bank that knowingly conducts or facilitates significant transactions tied to trade with North Korea or certain designated persons. The E.O. also enables Treasury to target any person conducting significant trade in goods, services, or technology with North Korea, and to ban them from accessing the U.S. financial system.

The Treasury Department actively investigates individuals and entities that are providing support to North Korea, including Chinese individuals and entities. I cannot comment on timing for the next round of designations, but I will note that the Treasury Department is committed to designating any individual or entity that is providing support to North Korea. We will use all of our authorities to act when we see instances of individuals and entities providing support to North Korea. Additionally, Treasury prefers to maintain flexibility in our sanctions targeting, especially in our ongoing dialogue with the Chinese government, which is limited when North Korea-related sanctions statutes call for mandatory sanctions on those continuing to engage with North Korea.

4. Some experts assert that Beijing is playing a "double game" whereby they agree to certain sanctions at the U.N. but then fail to enforce them. Meanwhile, as other countries do take actions to cut off ties with North Korea, China simply picks up the slack. China has a responsibility to be transparent and provide the international community with detailed, real-time information about their trade with North Korea. Crude oil appears to be North Korea's largest import from China, but China stopped reporting crude oil shipments in 2014. China is North Korea's gateway to the world -- what are we doing to hold China accountable for providing real-time data transparency on both sanctions enforcement as well as their "licit" trade with North Korea?

Answer:

Under the current UN sanctions regime, UN Member States are prohibited from importing coal, iron, iron ore, lead and seafood. Exports of raw crude and petroleum are capped. North Korean overseas labor is restricted. North Korean banks are cut off from the international financial system, and also are prohibited from maintaining representatives abroad.

Executive Order 13810 gives Treasury the authority to target any anyone conducting significant trade in goods, services, or technology with North Korea. We are using all the data available to the U.S. government to detect North Korea's sanctions evasion. We are mapping their illicit networks. We are investigating any individuals and entities that continue to trade with North Korea.

We have already demonstrated that we are willing to target companies trading with North Korea. For example in June and August Treasury designated individuals and companies involved in selling petroleum to North Korea. We have already demonstrated that we are willing to target companies trading with North Korea. For example in June and August Treasury designated individuals and companies involved in selling petroleum to North Korea. We will continue to do so as we dedicate staff resources to meet competing requirements to research, draft, review, and submit all of the periodic reports required by North Korea-related sanctions statutes.

5. Two of China's poorest provinces, Liaoning and Jilin, border North Korea, and China has put forward trade with North Korea as a path to greater economic growth. Today, the development plan for the provinces lay out policies designed increase trade with North Korea. At a time when the international community is trying to cut off sources of hard currency to the Kim Regime, is it reasonable to expect compliance from officials in Northeastern China? Given Beijing's concerns about stability, is it not more likely that the central government will look the other way and allow cross-border trade to continue?

Answer:

We expect the Chinese to comply with UN Security Council Resolutions. Executive Order 13810 put individuals and entities, including banks, on notice that they must choose between doing business with North Korea and doing business with the United States.

We recognize that China-North Korea trade occurs along the border, but we expect that China will crack down on this trade. Moreover, we have used sanctions targeted at the activity occurring in this region to specifically highlight to China that it disrupt this activity. On August 22, Treasury designated Chinese companies for importing North Korean coal and other UNSCR-prohibited items like vanadium. Four of these companies were located in Liaoning Province. On June 29, pursuant to Section 311 of the USA Patriot Act, Treasury found Bank of Dandong to be of "primary money laundering concern" and issued a notice of proposed rulemaking which, if finalized, would essentially cut Bank of Dandong off from the U.S. financial system. Bank of Dandong is also based in Liaoning Province. We will not hesitate to target any individual and entity that continues to trade with North Korea.6.   Some experts are calling for sudden and overwhelming economic pressure on North Korea – such as China cutting off oil to the Regime – to serve as a kind of "shock therapy." Would a sudden and overwhelming increase in economic pressure on North Korea be possible? Would it be advisable? How might the North Korean regime respond to such pressure?

Answer:

Our goal is to put maximum economic pressure on North Korea. We assess that North Korea is dependent on imports of both raw crude and petroleum and that constraining and cutting off their access to these resources would increase economic pressure on the regime. It is precisely for that reason that the US Government pushed for a UN Security Council Resolution that targets crude and oil. UNSCR 2375 puts a cap on countries' exports of oil and refined petroleum to North Korea, which is a first step.

We are already working in coordination with our allies to further reduce North Korea's supply of oil. In 2017, Treasury designated Russian individuals who were operating Singapore-based companies and selling gasoil to North Korea. These designations reinforce our commitment to ending all trade with North Korea, including the exportation of petroleum and crude. On October 16, the European Union announced a total ban on the sale of refined petroleum and crude oil to North Korea. We commend the EU for this new measure and we will continue pressing allies around the world to adopt similar restrictions.

I would be happy to discuss in a classified setting additional aspects to this important matter.

Questions for the Record Submitted to
Acting Assistant Secretary Thornton by
Representative Ami Bera
House Foreign Affairs Committee
September 12, 2017

Question:

Trade with China makes up about 90% of total North Korean trade. China has signed on to UN sanctions aimed at restricting North Korean access to cash and weapons, but have been circumventing the sanctions through several avenues, including "livelihood exemptions." What is the administration's plan for holding Chinese entities accountable for Sino-North Korean business transactions that violate existing sanctions? What metrics will the administration use to determine when more secondary sanctions are necessary and how broad those measures should be?

Answer:

Over 90% of the DPRK's exports go through or to China. That gives China significant economic leverage. That is why we have told the Chinese that Beijing's willingness to cooperate with us to solve the Asia Pacific region's most acute threat to peace and stability will be a benchmark of its commitment to pursue constructive, results-oriented relations with the United States. If it so chooses, China's use of its leverage over the DPRK could be a highlight of our bilateral cooperation. We welcome the positive steps that China has taken since the adoption of UNSCRs 2371 and 2375 to implement these resolutions. We want to see China fulfill its obligations completely and are hopeful that this additional economic pressure will change the calculus of the North Korea regime.

We have told the Chinese clearly and repeatedly that we will use all tools at our disposal, including U.S. sanctions, to choke off resources that fund the DPRK's proscribed nuclear, ballistic missile, and other WMD programs. We want to work with China, but we have said many times that we will not hesitate to act alone, including by sanctioning Chinese or other third-country individuals and entities that provide support to North Korea's unlawful activities.

The Administration will go wherever the evidence leads to impose legally available sanctions on entities or individuals that support North Korea's proscribed programs.

Question:

Ms. Thornton, while we seek the cooperation of China to pressure North Korea, we have traditionally confronted them on a variety of fronts, including over the South China Sea, human rights, and sometimes trade. Many of our allies abroad, and Americans at home, are rightfully worried over the sometimes seemingly transactional approach to diplomacy the administration has. How has our desire for cooperation with China impacted the other aspects of our relationship with that country? As the Assistant Secretary responsible for East Asia, how does

North Korea impact your own policy recommendations to Secretary Tillerson for areas outside of North Korea?

Answer:

This Administration has laid out a vision for U.S.-China relations that is constructive and results-oriented. In furthering this relationship, we are expanding areas of cooperation on issues where we have shared interests. But we also address, directly and very frankly, areas where we face threats or areas where we have differences so that we can narrow these differences and solve the problems. The U.S.-China relationship is one of the most consequential and broadest relationships the United States has in the world. We will – and must – be able to make progress in multiple areas. But will not turn a blind eye to problems that undermine American security or prosperity simply because China – or any country – is cooperating with us elsewhere.

Question

When North Korea obtains the ability to strike the U.S. homeland with a nuclear weapon, our allies immediately start to doubt the veracity of the U.S. nuclear umbrella. When choosing to defend Seoul at the cost of Los Angeles, the risk for the U.S. is clearly far higher if we chose to honor our commitments. In Europe, the U.S. was able to reassure our allies by making certain commitments under NATO, but there is no equivalent to NATO in Asia. Our "hub and spokes" alliance structure means there is greater risk that South Korea and Japan will explore their own means of defense independent from U.S. security commitments.

What is the administration doing to reassure our allies?

With no Ambassador in Seoul, what are we saying to the South Koreans?

Have we taken steps to elevate our dialogues on extended deterrence with South Korea and Japan?

Answer:

The President's top priority remains protecting the homeland, U.S. territories, and our allies against the threat posed by North Korea. We remain fully committed to the defense of our allies, the Republic of Korea (ROK) and Japan, and our commitments are backed by the full range of our conventional and nuclear capabilities, including extended deterrence. We view these commitments as both ironclad and durable.

In light of these commitments and in the face of continued DPRK provocations, we deployed a Terminal High Altitude Air Defense (THAAD) Battery to the ROK. We continue to rapidly deploy a broad range of strategic capabilities to the region in preparing to respond to, defend against, and if necessary defeat any DPRK attack – whether on the United States, South Korea, or Japan – with immediate, effective, and overwhelming force.

We want to be clear to the North Korean regime that the United States has the unquestionable ability to defend itself and its allies. As we and others have made clear, we will never accept a nuclear-armed North Korea nor abandon our commitments to our allies and partners in the region.

We are reassuring our ROK allies that our bilateral relationship remains a high priority. Secretary Tillerson has had multiple phone and face-to-face conversations with ROK Foreign Minister Kang, and leaders of the Administration at all levels have taken the opportunity to engage with their ROK counterparts.

Question:

Relations between Japan and South Korea have cooled in recent months. Given the urgency of the North Korea situation, it would seem to make sense to repair the relationship.

How would you characterize the level of Japan-South Korea- U.S. cooperation?
What steps are we taking to enhance all aspects of the relationship?

Answer:

The United States values our robust and productive trilateral relationship with Japan and the Republic of Korea. The United States, Japan, and the Republic of Korea (ROK) continue to engage regularly to remain in close coordination in response to the North Korea threat. The United States is steadfast in its defense commitments to the Republic of Korea and Japan, including the commitment to provide extended deterrence, backed by the full range of our nuclear and conventional defense capabilities. President Trump met trilaterally with Japanese Prime Minister Abe and ROK President Moon in Hamburg and, most recently, in New York on the margins of the UN General Assembly. Secretary Tillerson also met trilaterally with his Japanese and ROK counterparts in Bonn and Manila. Our continuous engagement at the highest levels of our government is a testament to the importance of our trilateral cooperation.

While historical issues continue to affect ROK-Japan bilateral relations, our two allies recognize the significant value of our trilateral cooperation as we seek to counter the North Korean threat and enhance not only our security cooperation, but also our global cooperation. Both Japanese Prime Minister Abe and ROK President Moon have committed publicly to pursue a future-oriented ROK-Japan bilateral relationship.

Questions for the Record Submitted to
Mr. Marshall Billingslea
House Foreign Affairs Committee
"Sanctions, Diplomacy, and Information: Pressuring North Korea"
September 12, 2017

<u>**Representative Ami Bera**</u>

1. Trade with China makes up about 90% of total North Korean trade. China has signed on to UN sanctions aimed at restricting North Korean access to cash and weapons, but have been circumventing the sanctions through several avenues, including "livelihood exemptions."

    What is the administration's plan for holding Chinese entities accountable for Sino-North Korean business transactions that violate existing sanctions?

    Answer:
    North Korea is an important issue in our bilateral relationship with China, as China accounts for more than 90 percent of North Korea's trade. Not only is North Korea a shared security concern, its illicit financial activity threatens the integrity of both the U.S. and Chinese financial systems.

    We are having direct conversations with China on how to work together to denuclearize the peninsula and implement the UN Security Council resolutions. Our preference is to work with China, but if necessary, Treasury can and will act unilaterally to impede illicit activity and protect the U.S. financial system from abuse.

    On June 29 and on August 22, Treasury designated Chinese individuals and entities involved in importing North Korean coal in support of the North Korean government, importing North Korean minerals in violation of UN Security Council Resolutions, or for providing financial services to North Korean banks. Additionally, on June 29 Treasury took steps to prevent China-based Bank of Dandong from continuing to serve as a gateway for North Korea to access the U.S. and international financial system by issuing a Notice of Propose Rulemaking pursuant to Section 311 of the USA PATRIOT Act.

    These designations and our 311 action show our resolve to target Chinese sanctions evasion and economic support to North Korea.

2. What metrics will the administration use to determine when more secondary sanctions are necessary and how broad those measures should be?

    Answer:
    U.S. sanction programs generally block the assets under U.S. jurisdiction of a foreign individual or entity engaged in enumerated activity, prohibiting U.S. persons from dealing with the sanctions target. "Secondary correspondent account sanctions" can be interpreted as severing or restricting foreign financial institutions' access to the U.S.

financial system for knowingly dealing with the U.S. sanctions targets or engaging in other enumerated activities.

On September 20, the President issued new Executive Order (E.O.) 13810, greatly expanding Treasury's sanctions authorities and expressly authorizing Treasury to use secondary correspondent account sanctions in the North Korea program. For example, E.O. 13810 authorizes Treasury to suspend or restrict U.S. correspondent account access to any foreign bank that knowingly conducts or facilitates significant transactions tied to trade with North Korea or certain designated persons. These sanctions will be forward looking, applicable to behavior that occurs after the issuance of the E.O. Additionally, the E.O. authorizes Treasury to designate any person that has engaged in at least one significant importation or exportation to North Korea of any goods, services, or technology. The international community and foreign financial institutions are now on notice that, going forward, they can choose to do business with the United States or with North Korea, but not both.

We will carefully monitor foreign financial institutions to ensure that they are living up to UN obligations and not knowingly conducting or facilitating significant transactions in connection with trade with North Korea or on behalf of UN- and U.S.- designated persons. We will let facts lead us to any future decisions we make. We must be judicious, strategic, and targeted in how we use our powerful authorities. Overall, the most crucial "metrics" we apply are the assessments of how effective the USG's actions have been at denying revenue to the DPRK, and introducing changes
in behavior with North Korean trading partners.

3. Notwithstanding recent designations, we still have a long way to go before we are exerting "maximum pressure" on North Korea's economic interests. The organization C4ADS and other open-source researchers have demonstrated that there is a centralized, limited and vulnerable network of third-party gateway firms in China and elsewhere that form North Korea's illicit network. One now-sanctioned Chinese firm (Dandong Hongxiang Industrial Development Co. Ltd.) used shell companies to process more than $70 million in transactions through the U.S. financial system.

Assistant Secretary Billingslea, can the U.S. identify the top 20-30 firms that compose North Korea's illicit network? It is my understanding that most of these entities operate in China and a small number of other jurisdictions.

Have we informed Beijing (and/or the relevant governments) of the activities of these entities and unequivocally communicated the expectation of the U.S. government that their actions be curbed?

Answer:
Treasury leadership regularly engages with their Chinese counterparts on working together to implement and enforce UN Security Council Resolutions and end funding
and facilitation to the North Korean regime.If those activities are classified, would you be willing to offer a detailed accounting of all the cases in which the U.S. raised the activities with the Chinese (and/or relevant governments)?

Answer:

At Treasury we have had very specific conversations with our Chinese counterparts, as well as other government interlocutors, with respect to entities that we believe are associated with the North Korean regime, and we have made very specific requests for action on these entities. There are also times, depending on the sensitivity of the target, we choose not to engage with other governments and instead take unilateral action.

Nevertheless, time is not on our side. North Korea is rapidly advancing its weapons programs. The current UN sanctions regime prohibits countries from importing most North Korean goods and commodities. We are pushing China to conduct a widespread crackdown on trade with North Korea. We are pushing the Chinese government to ensure that Chinese banks are not holding accounts for North Korean financial facilitators.

4. If Beijing (and/or the relevant governments) has not taken sufficient action to close these entities and curb their activities, has our government taken action to designate these entities under U.S. law and if not, what is the impediment to doing so?

Answer:

In August, Treasury designated three coal companies involved in importing nearly half a billion dollars' worth of North Korean coal between 2013 and 2016. At least one of those companies, Dandong Zhicheng, used shell companies to transfer funds through the U.S. financial system. On the same day as Treasury's designations, the Department of Justice issued a complaint for forfeiture to seize 4 million USD.

These actions reinforce that Treasury is committed to using our authorities under U.S. law to designate entities that provide any economic support to North Korea.

Question for the Record Submitted to
Assistant Secretary Thornton
by Representative Wagner
House Foreign Affairs Committee
September 12, 2017

Question:

Assistant Secretary Thornton, the United States must demonstrate leadership in ending North Korean slave labor and extracting commitments from countries worldwide to end the employment of North Korean workers and payments to the Kim regime. The September UN sanctions exempted existing contracts and work authorizations involving North Korean workers; to what degree will these exemptions impact the flow of payments to the regime? And by when will the existing authorizations expire?

      a. I appreciated your witness statement. You wrote that we have not seen any indication that the Kim regime is open to serious engagement. Barring a threat to the Kim regime's very survival, it will never give up its nuclear weapons. I'm not talking about regime change efforts; I'm talking about changing Kim's financial calculus. How does the U.S. propose to do that without the full inclusion of oil in UN resolutions?

      b. What is the United States doing to bring Kim Jong-un to the International Criminal Court for crimes against humanity?

Answer:

There is a unified international voice echoing our messages for greater pressure on the DPRK. The Security Council spoke clearly following the September 6 nuclear test to condemn North Korea's reckless and dangerous behavior, and we call on all nations to use every means of influence to make clear to the DPRK that further provocations are unacceptable.

With respect to your question about changing Kim's financial calculus, we are encouraged by the prompt adoption of UNSCR 2375, a resolution that includes the strongest sanctions ever imposed on North Korea, and introduces a partial ban on oil for the first time. We will continue to work with our diplomatic partners to ensure that this and previous UNSCRs on the DPRK are fully implemented. The UNSCR 2375 ban on textiles and overseas laborers alone will cut off $1.3 billion of revenue each year to the North Korean regime. Further, as we've made clear, we will not hesitate to act alone. On September 21, President Trump issued a new executive order with respect to North Korea, authorizing the United States to impose sanctions on persons involved in at least one significant importation from or exportation to North Korea of any goods, services, or technology. The Administration intends to make full use of these new authorities.

UNSCR 2375 does not proscribe an end date for existing DPRK labor contracts. Therefore, we will continue coordinating with like-minded nations to pressure countries still hosting DPRK laborers to cancel these contracts and expel DPRK overseas laborers as soon as possible.

Finally, the plight of the Korean people suffering at the hands of the Kim regime continues to be a major concern. We support Security Council consideration of the Commission of Inquiry report and its recommendations, including consideration of the recommendation that Kim Jung Un's situation be referred to the International Criminal Court. Our efforts are focused on continuing to shine a spotlight on North Korea's widespread and serious human rights violations and to lay the groundwork for holding those most responsible for these violations to account.

We continue to co-sponsor tough resolutions at the UN General Assembly and Human Rights Council stressing the importance of accountability. We have also taken domestic action, including naming and designating for sanctions over 30 persons, including Kim Jong Un, for being responsible for or associated with serious human rights abuses in the DPRK.

Questions for the Record Submitted to
Mr. Marshall Billingslea
House Foreign Affairs Committee
"Sanctions, Diplomacy, and Information: Pressuring North Korea"
September 12, 2017

<u>**Representative Ann Wagner**</u>

1. Thank you, Mr. Chairman, for hosting this timely hearing. In August, I traveled to Korea, Japan, and China to better understand current events on the Peninsula and dialogue with our allies. I had the opportunity to visit not only the DMZ, but also Dandong, where I watched Chinese trucks loaded with goods drive across the China-Korea Friendship Bridge into North Korea. 70% of North Korea's trade passes over that bridge, and it was a stark reminder that the United States should prioritize secondary sanctions against the Chinese companies and banks that sustain the regime.

   Assistant Secretary Billingslea, what steps is the Administration taking to levy secondary sanctions against every foreign company or bank funding the Kim regime? Why are we not seeing more secondary sanctions? When can we expect to see a comprehensive list?

   Answer:
   Subsequent to my testimony, the Treasury has sanctioned multiple North Korean banks and a substantial number of their financial intermediaries. On June 29, pursuant to Section 311 of the USA Patriot Act, Treasury found Bank of Dandong to be of "primary money laundering concern" and issued a notice of proposed rulemaking which, if finalized, would essentially cut Bank of Dandong off from the U.S. financial system.

   To employ secondary sanctions under Executive Order 13810, we must have clear evidence that a bank "knowingly" facilitated any significant transaction in connection with a North Korean entity, subsequent to when the order was signed. We are carefully monitoring the behavior of a wide range of financial institutions, and will not hesitate to act when the evidentiary threshold is met and our national security would be enhanced by the action.

Question for the Record Submitted to
Assistant Secretary Thornton by
Representative Brad Schneider
House Foreign Affairs Committee
September 12, 2017

In the July 5th call with Egyptian President Sisi, President Trump emphasized that Egypt should "stop hosting North Korean guest workers and stop providing economic or military benefits to North Korea." Egypt is the second largest recipient of U.S. security assistance.

Question:

What does Egypt get out of its relationship with North Korea that is worth risking their partnership with the United States?

Answer:

Egypt's foreign relations are based on its own assessments of national priorities and national interests. Cairo has had a longstanding relationship with North Korea, including military cooperation.

There is also a direct Egyptian economic investment in excess of half a billion dollars in North Korea. We would be happy to provide more comprehensive information in a classified briefing.

Question:

What is the Administration doing to press upon the Egyptians the importance of severing ties with North Korea?

Answer:

We have raised our concerns about North Korea, and Cairo's continued relationship with it, with the Egyptians repeatedly and at the highest levels. We also made it clear that Egypt's ties with the DPRK are a major concern when the Secretary decided in August to issue a national security waiver for $195 million in FY 2016 Foreign Military Funds (FMF), but hold availability of these funds pending positive Egyptian steps and also reprogrammed away from Egypt $65.7 million in FMF and $30 million of Economic Support Fund (ESF) funds. We believe that the reprogramming of these funds will reinforce U.S. concerns regarding Egyptian policies that run counter to our national interests and underscore the importance of Egypt's responsiveness to key U.S. asks without undermining Egypt's ability to fight ISIS and other threats to its security.

Questions for the Record Submitted to
Mr. Marshall Billingslea
House Foreign Affairs Committee
"Sanctions, Diplomacy, and Information: Pressuring North Korea"
September 12, 2017

<u>**Representative Brad Schneider**</u>

In the July 5th call with Egyptian President Sisi, President Trump emphasized that Egypt should "stop hosting North Korean guest workers and stop providing economic or military benefits to North Korea." Egypt is the second largest recipient of U.S. security assistance.

1. What does Egypt get out of its relationship with North Korea that is worth risking their partnership with the United States?

    Answer:
    The current relationship between Egypt and North Korea is unacceptable. We have made it clear to allies around the world that they must choose between doing business with North Korea or with the United States. We are prepared to reinforce that message through our designations. I also have reinforced that message recently with my Egyptian counterparts.

2. What is the Administration doing to press upon the Egyptians the importance of severing ties with North Korea?

    Answer:
    Treasury leadership discusses the threat posed by North Korea with our counterparts on a daily basis. The need to impose maximum economic pressure on North Korea is discussed in meetings with leaders from Africa, Asia, Europe, and the Middle East. That includes our engagement with Egypt as well as bilateral engagement conducted by the State Department.